ROYAL SCHOOL OF NEEDLEWORK

HANDBOOK OF EMBROIDERY (1880)

By

LETITIA HIGGIN

Edited by

LADY MARIAN ALFORD

With an introductory essay by

LYNN HULSE

Published by the Royal School of Needlework
Apartment 12A
Hampton Court Palace
East Molesey
Surrey KT8 9AU

www.royal-needlework.org.uk

Project managed by Michael Wicks
Printed by Quddos
Set in Caslon

ISBN: 978-0-9566455-0-0

Front and back covers: George Aitchison, Floral design,
'To the School of Art Needlework Princes Gate S Kensington
26 October 1876'

RSN Archive D2, fol. 27v. © Royal School of Needlework 2010,
photography Michael Wicks

Inside front cover: Letitia Higgin, *Handbook of Embroidery*
(London, 1880)
cover 1

Inside back cover: Letitia Higgin, *Handbook of Embroidery*
(London, 1880)
cover 2

CONTENTS

*The blank pages found in the appendix to the original text (pp [65]–[96]) have been omitted in the facsimile edition.

LIST OF FIGURES

Fig. 11 Embroidery frame from Anastasia Dolby, *Church Embroidery Ancient and Modern* (London, 1867), plate 18. © Royal School of Needlework 2010, photography Michael Wicks

Fig. 12 RSN workroom, Exhibition Road, c1903. RSN Archive 122/33. © Royal School of Needlework 2010, photography Lynn Hulse

Fig. 13 Christiana Cresswell, *Vine* curtain, mid-1870s. RSN Archive D7. © Royal School of Needlework 2010, photography Michael Wicks

Fig. 14 Three-panel Oriental screen, designed and embroidered by Mary Gemmell, c1876, from Walter Smith, *Examples of Household Taste* (New York, [1877]), p. 372. National Art Library, photography Lynn Hulse

Fig. 15 Selwyn Image, Cushion cover, designed for the prepared work department of the RSN, 1880s, detail. RSN Textile temporary no. 10. © Royal School of Needlework 2010, photography Lynn Hulse

Figs 16a–b Designs supplied by the Royal School of Art Needlework, supplement to *The Queen*, 16 July 1881 and 11 February 1882. RSN Archive D3. © Royal School of Needlework 2010, photography Michael Wicks

Fig. 17 *Hand-Book of Embroidery* (Boston, 1883). Private collection, photography Michael Wicks

Fig. 18 Edward Burne-Jones, *Musica*, embroidered by the RSN, undated. Private Collection, © Image Bridgeman Art Library

Fig. 19 Edward Burne-Jones, *Poesis*, embroidered by the RSN, 1880. National Gallery of Victoria, Melbourne, Australia. Purchased through the Art Foundation of Victoria with the assistance of Miss Flora MacDonald Anderson and Mrs Ethel Elizabeth Ogilvy Lumsden Founder Benefactors, 1992 (CT1-1992)

Fig. 20 Walter Crane, *Complete Design for Decorating a Room with Hangings* from Walter Smith, *Examples of Household Taste* (New York, [1877]), p. 177. National Art Library, photography Lynn Hulse

Figs 21a–b Walter Crane, preparatory designs for the *Elements* screen, late 1870s. Local Studies Department, Kensington Central Library, Crane Portfolios F(1)/18 and G(6)/39. Royal Borough of Kensington and Chelsea Library Service, photography Lynn Hulse

Fig. 22 Walter Crane, *Elements* screen, embroidered by the RSN, *c*1879. © V&A Images/Victoria and Albert Museum, London

Figs 23a–b Pair of panels based on Walter Crane's design for the *Elements* screen, probably embroidered by the RSN in the late 1870s. © Paul Reeves

Figs 24a–b Walter Crane, *Daffodil* and *Primrose*, *c*1876. RSN Archive D6/9-10. © Royal School of Needlework 2010, photography Michael Wicks

Fig. 25 George Aitchison, Floral design 'embroidered on blue satin', 7 October 1876. RSN Archive D2, fol. 28. © Royal School of Needlework 2010, photography Michael Wicks

Fig. 26 Royal School of Art Needlework, architect Fairfax B Wade, 1903. RSN Archive 122/1. © Royal School of Needlework 2010, photography Michael Wicks

Fig. 27 Fairfax B Wade, *Forget-me-not* design, November 1874. RSN Archive D2, fol. 16r. © Royal School of Needlework 2010, photography Michael Wicks

Fig. 28 Hanging stitched by Lady Emily Plowden, undated. Reproduced by permission of the Victoria and Albert Museum, photography Lynn Hulse

Figs 29a–b Selwyn Image, *Juno* and *Minerva*, embroidered by the RSN, *c*1879. Private collection, © Image Patch Rogers

Fig. 30 Selwyn Image, *Venus*, embroidered by the RSN, undated. Private collection, © Image Sotheby's

Fig. 31 Helen Marion Burnside, *Magnolia*, undated. RSN Archive D5/39. © Royal School of Needlework 2010, photography Lynn Hulse

ACKNOWLEDGEMENTS

I am grateful to the Earl of Wemyss and to Sir Bruno Welby, Bt for their generosity in granting access and permission to publish material from their family papers.

I would like to thank the following for their generous assistance in the preparation of this volume: past and present staff of the RSN, in particular Susan Kay-Williams, Eva Hansson, Owen Davies, Nicola Jarvis, Becky Hogg, Nicky Hooper, Helen McCook, Helen Stevens and Adele Lindridge; Edwina Ehrman, Curator of Nineteenth Century Textiles and Fashion, Victoria & Albert Museum; Max Donnelly, Fine Art Society, London; Adrian James, Assistant Librarian, Society of Antiquaries of London; Victoria Osborne, Curator of Prints and Drawings, Birmingham Museums and Art Gallery; David Smith, Archivist, Berkeley Castle; Berkeley Will Trust; Eileen Simpson, Archivist to the Grosvenor Estate; the Trustees of the 4th Duke of Westminster's 1964 Settlement; Adrian Wilkinson, Collections Officer, Lincolnshire Archives; Kathy Woodrell, Reference Specialist, Decorative Arts, Library of Congress, Washington DC; Charles E Greene, Librarian, Manuscripts, Rare Books & Special Collections, Princeton University; Stephen Price; Linda Parry; Mary Schoeser; Brenda King; Elizabeth Kramer; Meg Andrews; Paul Petzold; Bill Barnes; Sue Bodinetz; the staff at the National Art Library (Victoria & Albert Museum), the National Archives, the Royal Institute of British Architects, the Royal Borough of Kensington & Chelsea, Family & Children's Service and the Bridgeman Art Library; Paul Reeves (Paul Reeves Furniture and Artefacts 1860-1960); Sotheby's Auctioneers; Patch Rogers (Arts and Crafts Design 1850-present day, www.acfc.co.uk); Helen Dunstan (Haslam and Whiteway); Jennie Moloney, Scheduling and Copyright Coordinator, National Gallery of Victoria, Melbourne, Australia; Revinder Chahal, V&A Images; and Angela Lassig, Senior Curator, Te Papa Tongarewa, Wellington, New Zealand.

I am indebted to Michael Wicks for photographing the *Handbook* and for typesetting and overseeing the printing of the facsimile edition.

I should like to acknowledge the financial support of the RSN's legacy donor and the Marc Fitch Fund, which provided a research grant towards the cost of illustrations.

From: HRH The Duchess of Gloucester, GCVO
        President, Royal School of Needlework

Ever since mankind found the need to wear clothes the use of the needle has developed beyond the practical, to become an expression of decorative creativity.

In 1872 the Royal School of Needlework was founded to protect that creativity from the threat of mechanisation, particularly from overseas. To show that this ambition could be sharply focused, the Royal School resolved to print a Handbook in order to demonstrate both its policy and its methodology, by means of clear diagrams of approved stitches and approved contemporary designs for its readers to copy.

The designs have moved on, yet the stitches remain universal and thus render this historic document relevant to today's needlework and to the direction taken by the Royal School.

As their President, I am delighted to commend Dr Lynn Hulse's fine introduction which sets the scene so that the reader can see the content in its true context.

FOREWORD

It is 130 years since the *Handbook of Embroidery* was first published by the Royal School of Needlework (RSN) in order to establish the recently formed school as the centre of learning for the practical and technical aspects of the stitch. The five chapters on fabrics, equipment and stitches make interesting, and still useful, reading. Furthermore, they provide a window into the significant contribution made by the RSN to the revival of art embroidery and the development of textile manufacture in the 1870s. But the special aspects of this book are actually after the sixty or so pages of instruction: first the designs by William Morris, Edward Burne-Jones, Selwyn Image, Walter Crane *et al* show not only the way the RSN worked with contemporary designers, but the high place that art embroidery held among the decorative arts in the last quarter of the nineteenth century. Secondly, the section on the RSN itself, including committees, prospectus, classes and the range of work undertaken, reveals a world of embroidered bath blankets, opera cloaks and my particular favourite, the tennis apron, now long gone.

So the facsimile of the *Handbook* will be of interest to social, textile, design and economic historians even without the fascinating introduction by Dr Lynn Hulse. Here we have a new insight into the history of the RSN thanks in no small part to Lynn's detective abilities to discover where materials from our long history now reside and gain the support of the current custodians to examine the papers and finished commissions. We are very grateful to them for their assistance.

As a result of her extensive research, Lynn has brought new light to the question of why there was only one edition of the *Handbook*; how the RSN sowed the seed for the development of art needlework in the USA; and the precarious nature of the first years of the RSN. The introduction corrects inaccuracies in previous publications and fills in several gaps in the available knowledge of the RSN's first decade. The reason for this gap in the literature was that for decades the archives of the RSN have been hidden in cupboards, and for the last twenty years behind the thick walls of Hampton Court Palace, making access, even for researchers, rather difficult. So, the decision to print the facsimile and introduction is part of a wider programme to make the RSN's history better known, drawing on the extensive, though inevitably incomplete, archives. This short introduction cannot, though give the full picture and it will take another work to address fully the early history of the RSN, but it does offer a valuable beginning.

I would also like to pay tribute to Nik Rochez, Hon Treasurer of the RSN, who, with a small team of trustees, has overseen this publication, and to our legacy donor who has helped provide the initial funds, ensuring that this facsimile edition has just as interesting a story in how it came to be produced as the first edition.

The RSN is now the only one of the nineteenth-century British embroidery organisations still in existence. We remain, still teaching the art and techniques of hand embroidery to the highest standard and still providing a UK-based Studio for new commissions and restoration/conservation. But this does not mean we have ossified. Instead the last few years have seen the most significant developments in the RSN's history for many decades with the launch of the Foundation Degree in hand embroidery and the Diploma in technical hand embroidery, to be followed by an MA in hand embroidery shortly. We have undertaken commissions for private individuals and celebrated artists to public bodies where thousands can appreciate our work, and we have launched new courses from Bristol to Tokyo and firmly established our US courses in San Francisco.

The Royal School of Needlework is an organisation with a great future and a long story yet to tell, but the facsimile of the *Handbook* and introduction shine a fascinating light on our early days.

Dr Susan Kay-Williams
Chief Executive

Fig. 1 Princess Helena, President of the RSN, attending the opening of the School's new premises on Exhibition Road in June 1875.

INTRODUCTION

The Royal School of Needlework (RSN) opened in November 1872 in a small room over a bonnet shop at 38 Sloane Street, Kensington, London.[1] The founder, Lady Victoria Welby,[2] believed that 'the universal substitution of printed or woven designs for hand-made decoration' had resulted in the decline of ornamental needlework in Britain. With missionary zeal, she set about reviving 'a beautiful and practically lost art', the superiority of which 'can scarcely be disputed'. Through this revival, the RSN would provide employment for distressed gentlewomen in reduced circumstances.[3]

The RSN was not the first embroidery school to do good works. With the increase in demand for church vestments and furnishings from the mid-nineteenth century onwards, impoverished ladies, willing to ply their needle, were assured a modest income from embroidery workrooms associated with the Anglican and Roman Catholic convents.[4] What set the RSN apart was its commitment to execute 'ornamental needlework for *secular* purposes' only.[5] Moreover, the RSN was the first school of its kind in Britain to secure the patronage of several prominent members of the ruling elite and the royal family whose active participation in the management of the institution added considerable prestige to the whole enterprise.[6]

Prospective employees were required to provide two references from respected members of society such as clergymen, doctors, lawyers, politicians, army officers and the aristocracy, to live within commuting distance of the RSN and be able and willing to work seven hours per day. Each applicant had to go through a course of instruction at a cost of £5 paid in advance or worked out at the discretion of the manageress. Training consisted of nine five-hour lessons in art needlework. On the satisfactory completion of the course, a certificate was issued and the applicant's name added to the list of qualified workers.[7]

Though only known to a circle of private friends, the RSN soon received a number of valuable commissions for new embroideries as well as requests to transfer, repair and copy antique needlework. Within two years of its foundation, the number of qualified workers had risen from twenty to eighty-eight plus twelve administrative staff. In order to meet the increased demand in business, the RSN moved into larger premises on the west side of Exhibition Road in June 1875 (Fig. 1).[8] By this time the School was divided into various departments, each run by a mistress and her assistant: a large general work room that executed 'varied work in all materials and styles'; an appliqué and gold work room; a crewel work room specially set apart to embroider the designs of William Morris, Walter Crane and others; a prepared work room that produced partially-worked kits for amateur embroiderers to stitch at home; a studio or paint room that composed, altered, traced, pricked and painted designs on behalf of the work rooms; and a showroom containing specimens of all the styles carried out.[9]

In January 1880 the RSN published its first needlework manual entitled *Handbook of Embroidery*, which the artist and designer Aymer Vallance later described as 'A work containing not only a summary of technical hints of the utmost value, but also some reproductions of designs of great beauty'.[10] The *Handbook* represents in microcosm the early history of the RSN and its relationship with many of the leading figures of the Aesthetic and Arts and Crafts Movements, a selection of whose designs are published in the Appendix to the original text. This introductory essay to the RSN's facsimile edition examines the *Handbook*'s contents in light of new research into the first decade of the School's operations and includes detailed entries on the twenty-five specimens of embroidery printed in the Appendix. The essay also explores the publishing history of this fascinating book and assesses its reception both at home and abroad during the late nineteenth century.

BACKGROUND TO THE PUBLICATION
OF THE HANDBOOK

Following a lengthy, heated debate on the management of the RSN during the spring and summer of 1877, several key members of staff, including the work room mistress, Elizabeth Gemmell, were dismissed as part of the re-organisation of the School.[11] By way of compensation, Lady Marian Alford, Vice-President of the RSN, invited Miss Gemmell to write a needlework manual, but she declined the offer.[12] Lady Welby shared Miss Gemmell's concern that 'she could not do [the book] well and informed Lady Alford that 'writing is <u>not</u> her forte, nor has she the requisite research in the subject'.[13]

Keen to advance the project, Lady Welby approached Mary Elliott Scrivenor, wife of a Lincolnshire clergyman, who managed The Society for the Employment of Ladies of Small Means from her home at St Mary's Vicarage, Horncastle.[14] The Society, which was renowned for its excellent needlework, had evolved from Mrs Scrivenor's lengthy association with the lady's newspaper, *The Queen*.[15] On 5 November 1877, Mrs Scrivenor wrote to Lady Welby expressing interest in the proposal:

> You said something about Lady Marion Alford offering to pay expenses of a work in Embroideries etc. If you think I am able to do it from what you have seen of my productions, I should not at all mind setting to work, and finishing what I have already begun. If I can get old specimens of work lent to me I could make it much more valuable[.] I feel sure it would meet with a sale for I am constantly asked to print in a separate form what I have already written and "the Plant" as it is called in Printers Phraseology has been offered to me by the Editor of the Queen, of all my own things and others, bearing on the subject.[16]

Before reaching a decision, Lady Alford wanted to learn more about Mrs Scrivenor's talents as a writer, and informed Lady Welby that she had received offers from two others ladies, 'so there is no lack of writers to choose from'.[17] Lady Welby assured Lady Alford that Mrs Scrivenor was 'far & away the best person to undertake [the book]… [having] the necessary gifts in an extraordinary degree'. Moreover, she knew from Mrs Scrivenor's recent communication that

…others are contemplating giving her the commission; & she is so practically well fitted for the book that I fear the appearance of her work would effectively supplant any other & it would be a great thing if the standard work on the subject should appear under our auspices.[18]

Despite Lady Welby's best endeavours to promote Mrs Scrivenor, the RSN did not invite her to author the book, nor does she appear to have completed such a work on behalf of *The Queen*.[19]

Several members of the RSN Council shared Lady Alford's desire to produce a needlework manual, but the project was not realised until the beginning of 1879 when Miss Higgin, the School's assistant secretary, submitted a manuscript on embroidery to the Managing Committee, the group of Council members responsible for overseeing the running of the institution.[20]

Letitia or Lily Higgin was born into a prominent Lancaster family on 20 November 1837.[21] She was the youngest child of Thomas Housman Higgin, deputy governor of Lancaster Castle, sometime mayor of the city and owner of the White Cross cotton mills.[22] Three of Higgin's daughters were employed at the RSN. Sarah Anne entered one of the work rooms in 1875 at the age of forty-four, but left within a few months, the work at a frame 'not agreeing with her'.[23] Martha, who was nine years older, first became a member of the showroom staff before moving to the stockroom and prepared work department.[24] Letitia joined the School in January 1876 to help Mary Haworth, the RSN secretary, but she was soon transferred to the post of manager's assistant. She was promoted to assistant secretary at the re-organisation of the RSN in the summer of 1877.[25] Miss Higgin proved to be a most competent worker; in February 1879, her salary was increased from £100 to £150 per annum.[26]

At a meeting held on 6 March 1879 the Managing Committee approved the manuscript, instructed Miss Higgin to find designs for the cover and gave directions to print the volume 'at once'.[27] Three weeks later Princess Helena — Queen Victoria's third daughter, wife of Prince Christian of Schleswig-Holstein and President of the RSN—formally requested Lady Alford to edit the text, which she agreed to do.[28] However, on reading through the manuscript Lady Alford found that it required 'a great deal of alteration', which she carried out while keeping as much as possible to the original structure of the book.[29]

Together Miss Higgin and Lady Alford entered into negotiations with the publisher and photographer Joseph Cundall (1818–1895), who had been responsible since 1866 for the publications and reproductions of the South Kensington Museum.[30] Cundall was also at the forefront of the systematic campaign to photograph works of art; the Bayeux Tapestry, for example, was photographed and published under his direction in 1875.[31] It was through him that the RSN signed a contract on 18 October 1879 with the London publisher Sampson Low & Co, one of the leading firms in the Victorian book trade.[32] The publisher's catalogue of general literature ranged from fiction to travel, geography, science, theology, music and the arts. Prior to the publication of the RSN volume, Sampson Low & Co had produced a handful of books on textiles, including Fanny Bury Palliser's *History of Lace* (1865; 2nd edn 1869; 3rd edn 1875), regarded as 'the classic work on the subject', and was therefore keen to acquire Miss Higgin's needlework manual.[33]

The *Handbook* was published jointly with the New York firm Scribner and Welford.[34] Founded in 1857 by the American publisher, Charles Scribner, and his partner, Charles Welford, son of a London bookseller, the business imported foreign books.[35] Welford had acquired considerable experience in this field, having previously been in partnership during the 1840s with the antiquarian book dealer John Russell Bartlett, who specialised in English works. In 1864, Welford moved to Britain to oversee the purchase of foreign books, setting up an office of Scribner and Welford in London in July 1878. The firm published a number of works in collaboration with Sampson Low & Co, thus the RSN book was assured a wide readership on both sides of the Atlantic.[36]

The publisher agreed to pay all the expenses involved in producing the *Handbook* and allowed a royalty to Lady Alford as the RSN's representative.[37] The volume was published on 17 January 1880 'by the authority of the Royal School of Art Needlework', and dedicated to its President, 'H.R.H. Princess Christian, of Schleswig-Holstein, Princess of Great Britain and Ireland'.[38] Priced at the reasonably high sum of 5s, the *Handbook* was soon advertised in the London and provincial press.[39]

PHYSICAL DESCRIPTION

The identity of the printer is recorded in the colophon that appears at the end of the *Handbook*: 'CHISWICK PRESS: C. WHITTINGHAM, TOOKS COURT, CHANCERY LANE'.[40] The London printer, Charles Whittingham (1767–1840), had established the press at Chiswick in the early nineteenth century. His nephew and namesake, who had set up a printing shop at 21 Tooks Court, off Chancery Lane in Holborn, took over the management of the Chiswick shop in 1839, inheriting the press outright the following year. Whittingham the younger (1795–1876) adopted the Chiswick Press imprint for his own books and from 1852 ran the business entirely from Tooks Court.[41] Considered the finest commercial printer of the nineteenth century, he was largely responsible for the revival in 1840 of the old face roman types designed by the type founder William Caslon (1692–1766) over a century before.[42] The *Handbook* is a typical example of the work produced by the Chiswick Press during and immediately after Whittingham's lifetime. The review published in *The Graphic* drew attention to the 'perspicuous and wonderfully clear' letterpress, set in Caslon type (which is also used in this introduction).[43]

Issued in octavo format, measuring 21cm in height by 14cm in width, the *Handbook* contains 61 leaves of high quality paper. The text block falls into three distinct sections:

1. The front matter, including half-title page, title page, preface (pp [v]–viii) and table of contents (pp [ix]–xii) followed by the needlework manual (pp [1]–60);
2. An appendix containing designs for embroidery ('Description of the Plates', pp [61]–64, plus 22 plates printed on a heavier weight paper, pp [65]–[96]); and
3. A brochure advertising the RSN (pp [97]–[108]).

Most extant copies of the *Handbook* are bound in pasteboard with plain brown endpapers and gold leaf applied to the head, tail and fore-edge of the leaves. Miss Higgin submitted a number of designs for the cover to the RSN's newly re-formed Art Committee, which consisted of a group of women with considerable experience in the fine and decorative arts. Mary Stuart Wortley (1848–1941), who was Lady Welby's cousin, had trained at the Slade School of Art, and during the last quarter of the nineteenth century, she exhibited paintings at the Royal Academy, the Grosvenor Gallery and elsewhere.[44] Fellow committee members Lady Alford and Mrs Madeline Wyndham (1835–1920), who was 'especially keen' on the School, were both accomplished watercolourists and embroiderers. The latter also worked in enamels and patronised many of the leading artists and designers connected with the Holland Park circle, who in turn were involved in the RSN.[45] All three ladies produced needlework designs for the School. (Fig. 2. The colour plates will be found from p. 83.)

At their first meeting held on 25 March 1879, the Art Committee chose one design for the cover,[46] though the *Handbook* was eventually published with two distinctly different designs printed on paper and pasted onto both the front and back boards. There is no evidence to suggest that the alternative cover is indicative of a reissue, for the text, including the title page and the front matter, is the same in both copies. The identity of the designer remains unknown. On the cover illustrated in Fig. 3 the title, *Handbook of Embroidery*, is printed in red and black letters and framed within a laurel wreath. The School motto, 'A little bird may fly high,' and the 'VR/RSAN' (Victoria Regina/Royal School of Art Needlework) monogram, designed by Lady Alford in the spring of 1875, link together four roundels displaying the changing role of women in mid-Victorian society and the contribution made by the RSN to promoting their training and employment.[47] The image of mother and child in the top left hand corner symbolises respectable domesticity, the 'angel in the house' embodied in Coventry Patmore's hugely popular poem on the Victorian feminine ideal.[48] However, by the 1870s women had already begun to assert their independence. Furthermore, needlework had broken free from the chains of manual dexterity, portrayed in the top right hand corner of the cover design, to reclaim 'the high place it once held among the decorative arts'.[49] Through the establishment of schools of embroidery, gentlewomen like those illustrated in the lower two roundels had access to a professional training in technique and design.[50] By the time the *Handbook* was published art decoration had become a suitable profession for women in that it provided them with a reasonable means of livelihood yet at the same time did not interfere with 'the present employment of men'.[51]

The second cover (Fig. 4), which bears the title *Royal School of Art Needlework Modern Embroidery*, features six pairs of courting swans in the Aesthetic style, reminiscent of Walter Crane's *Swan, Rush and Iris* wallpaper pattern (Victoria and Albert Museum no. E.17–1945), dating from 1875 (Fig. 5). According to one theory, the swan design was reserved for use only on work room copies of the *Handbook*, but there is no evidence to corroborate this view.[52] The volume was primarily a technical guide for amateur embroiderers, not professional needlewomen, and therefore was of limited use to the School's workers.[53] Moreover, there can be little doubt that this second cover with its reference to modern embroidery was intended to make a conspicuous statement about the RSN's commitment to contemporary design and its role as a prime mover in the recent development of art embroidery.

In the opinion of *The Queen*, the *Handbook* was 'profusely illustrated' with woodcut stitch diagrams, which Miss Higgin claimed to have designed 'in the rough' apart from two additions made by Miss Stuart Wortley.[54] At the request of Lady Alford, Miss Herbert designed the outline ornamental head and tailpieces found on several pages of the book.[55] Born in Queens County (now Co Laois), Ireland in *c*1858, Mary Herbert was the daughter of a civil engineer and granddaughter of Sir Frederick Pollock, Chief Baron of the Exchequer.[56] She had joined the paint room of the RSN in June 1878 in the company of her older sisters, Frances and Grace.[57] *The Times* thought her work admirable, comparing it to the 'embellishments which occur in profusion in [the] typographical masterpieces' of the Italian humanist and printer Aldus Manutius (1449/50–1515), founder of the Aldine Press at Venice, and recommended her designs to 'pliers of the needle who, tired with sprays of fruit, flowers, and leaves, prefer conventional designs' (Fig. 6).[58]

At a Managing Committee meeting on 27 June 1879, Lady Alford proposed a payment of £25 to the ladies involved in the preparation of the *Handbook*.[59] The Finance Committee approved the sum three weeks later; £20 was paid to Miss Higgin for drafting the text and £5 to Miss Herbert and the other ladies in the studio 'who had rendered assistance' in preparing the illustrations.[60]

The Art Committee chose for inclusion in the *Handbook* twelve specimens of embroidery demonstrating the wide range of designs made at the RSN.[61] There are no further records in the minutes regarding the specimens; however, by the time the volume was published the number included in the Appendix had more than doubled. *The Queen* noted that the designs, some of which had been photographed at the RSN by Sampson Low & Co (Fig. 7), were 'exceedingly well printed in colour and outline'.[62] The *Handbook* contains twenty-five photolithographs comprising ten black and white line images printed over a grey check or raster background to create tone (plates 1–2, 4–5, 8, 17–19) and fifteen colour images (plates 3, 6–7, 9–16, 20–22), produced by Vincent Brooks Day & Son.[63] Established in London in the early 1820s, Day & Son was one of the foremost lithographic firms of the mid-nineteenth century. Vincent Brooks (d. 1885), who took over the business in 1867, had already printed lithographs for Sampson Low & Co.[64] By the 1870s the firm was well known for its series of portrait caricatures produced for the popular weekly magazine *Vanity Fair*.[65]

Fig. 6 Mary Herbert, Ornamental head and tailpieces, from Letitia Higgin, *Handbook of Embroidery* (London, 1880), pp [1]-2.

THE NEEDLEWORK MANUAL

The Queen commented in its review of the *Handbook*:

We have often wondered why the Ladies of the Royal School of Art Needlework did not take the general public into their confidence with regard to the technical part of the embroiderer's art, in which they have been the acknowledged leaders for many years, and must have gained a thorough and varied experience./ Ample amends, however, have been made for this reticence by the excellent technical guide book just issued from the headquarters of decorative stitchery in Great Britain.[66]

According to the preface written by Lady Alford, the needlework manual was not intended to be a comprehensive encyclopaedia of embroidery stitches for the complete beginner. Written partly in response to the constant flow of enquiries received from amateur needlewomen, its aim was to supply useful hints to those 'unable to avail themselves of lessons, and are forced to puzzle over their difficulties without help from a trained and experienced embroiderer'. The volume was also designed for those ladies who had attended classes run by the RSN as an *aide memoire* of the 'many little details which might easily be forgotten when the lessons are over, though so much of the success of embroidery depends upon them.' Readers were assured that both author and editor had consulted 'all [the] acknowledged authorities' on the subject and had selected with the assistance of the RSN's teaching staff, 'the most practical and instructive' rules for inclusion in the volume.[67]

The *Handbook* was not the first manual published on the subject of art needlework. Three years earlier Miss Turner had produced a booklet entitled *Practical Hints on the Revived Art of Crewel and Silk Embroidery* (M A Turner & Co, London, 1877), which appeared in several editions. However, in the opinion of *The Queen*, 'This small manual…is written in such a cursory, not to say faulty manner, that we cannot think it will be of any use as a guide to those arts.'[68] Published the following year, M S Lockwood and Elizabeth Glaister's *Art Embroidery: A Treatise on the Revived Practice of Decorative Needlework* (Marcus Ward & Co, London and Belfast, 1878) focused less on technique and more on the subjects of design, composition and colour,[69] topics that Lady

Alford promised would appear shortly in the second part of the RSN *Handbook*. This prompted *The Queen* to comment:

> If the author succeeds in treating these more abstract subjects in an equally comprehensive and terse manner as the technical part of the task, both volumes will be indeed most valuable contributions to any lady's library.[70]

The Queen found Miss Higgin's book to be '[f]ull of practical hints, instructions, and directions, equally well arranged as clearly expressed' and pronounced that the volume deserved to take 'first place amongst the standard books on embroidery'.[71] The first two chapters contain information on the implements and materials available to the Victorian embroiderer as well as the textile fabrics 'best suited' as grounds for needlework (pp [1]–[18]). Chapters 3 and 5 include clear and concise instructions with diagrams of what the School regarded as the most useful stitches employed in hand and frame embroidery (pp [19]–32, [37]–58). Sandwiched in between is a chapter on framing with advice on 'the best and least fatiguing method of working' at a frame (pp [33]–36). The manual closes with a few hints on stretching, finishing and cleaning work (pp 59–60).

The technique for tracing designs onto fabric was deliberately omitted from the *Handbook*, partly because prior to 1881 the RSN only supplied patterns in the form of prepared work.[72] In the early 1870s, the preferred method practised by Lady Welby and Mrs Anastasia Dolby (*c*1824–1873),[73] the first superintendent of the School, was pricking and pouncing. By the end of the decade, the RSN had rejected this technique along with stamping and ironing from transfer papers, having found that 'designs can only be artistically and well traced on material by hand painting'.[74]

Threads and Fabric Grounds

Advice on threads and textile fabrics used as grounds for embroidery can be found in Miss Turner's *Practical Hints* and in Lockwood and Glaister's *Art Embroidery*, though neither publication contains the range of information printed in the *Handbook*.[75] While the manual is reticent on the significant contribution made by the RSN to developments in textile manufacture during the 1870s, Miss Higgin waxed lyrical on the subject in an article entitled 'Decorative Needlework', printed in *The Queen* one month after the publication of the *Handbook*.[76] She attributed several of the advances made in the production of crewels and silks to the tenacity of the RSN's 'little band of ladies' in reviving the art of decorative embroidery through the study of antique textiles. Initially the School had used carpet thrums or waste worsteds left over from weaving Brussels carpets for its crewel work, but found the threads coarse and uneven and the colours limited.[77] As the RSN's reputation for conserving and copying Stuart embroideries increased, thread manufacturers, including Appleton Bros, began to experiment with reproducing crewels based on old specimens found in country houses.[78] Crewels were widely available during the 1870s, but the RSN advised against using inferior threads dyed with fugitive aniline dyes that did not wash or clean and in some cases gave off 'a colouring matter to everything round about'.[79] According to the *Handbook*, the School preferred untwisted crewels of the best quality that allowed the colours, dyed with vegetable dyes that were 'perfectly fast', and bore repeated washing, to blend harmoniously. Furthermore, the RSN found crewels to be 'very effective' when combined with embroidery silk or filoselle in conventional designs or floral patterns, the leaves worked in crewels and the flowers in silk.[80]

Improvements were made in the manufacture and dyeing of silks in 1879–1880, partly in response to the demands of the RSN, which bought the bulk of its threads from Pearsall & Co and Adams.[81] The *Handbook* describes a range of silks, though the RSN preferred embroidery or bobbin silk to many of the others varieties on the market. In the opinion of Miss Higgin, purse silk had 'a hard, ridgy appearance', floss silk was 'always difficult to use, and [was] expensive and wasteful', and filoselle or spun silk was 'crude in colouring and fluffy in its nature'.[82] Vegetable-dyed bobbin silk was available in the 'richest and most delicate of ancient colours produced and rendered absolutely fast'. It was sold either as 'fine silk' in single strands or as 'rope silk' consisting of twelve strands, each with a slight twist 'to keep it from catching on every inequality of the finger and from fraying into a tangle'.[83]

The section on gold thread and its manufacture printed on pp 8–10 of the *Handbook* is based on the work of Mrs Dolby, who in turn was quoting from Frances Lambert's *The Hand-book of Needlework* (John Murray, London and Wiley & Putnam, New York, 1842).[84] The RSN manual is one of the earliest publications to discuss the use of Japanese gold thread, though according to

Miss Higgin, it was still extremely difficult to obtain *c*1880 despite the signing of the Treaty of Yedo, which had opened the way for trade relations between Britain and Japan over two decades earlier.[85] The *Handbook* reiterated the view expressed by several Victorian writers on needlework that English and French gold thread was tricky to work with particularly in London as 'damp and coal-smoke tarnish [it] almost before the work is out of the frame' in contrast to Japanese gold which never tarnished.[86] Anxious to secure the best materials available, Lady Welby presented a letter to the Japanese minister to London in 1873 begging him to 'give us all possible facilities for procuring gold thread, silk, &c from Japan'. The following year the RSN received from Yokohama a shipment of 30lbs of gold thread, valued at $120, and offered to sell part of the consignment on to other embroidery work rooms, including Tattersall & Co, who notified Lady Welby, 'we shall be glad to have 4 ounces, not too fine'.[87] By 1884, the RSN was supplying Japanese gold thread at 2s per skein.[88]

The *Handbook* also informed readers of new developments in the thread industry. Arrasene, a type of worsted chenille that had 'a very soft, rich appearance', is recommended for use on furnishings such as screen panels and borders where 'the highest class of art needlework' is required.[89] Miss Higgin was much taken with Thomas Wardle's experiments in the tussur (tasar, tassah) or 'wild silk' of India. She predicted that the soft and lustrous embroidery silks, produced for less than half the price of the cultivated silks from Italy, China and Japan, would create 'a revolution in embroidery' and become 'an important element in decorative needlework' (Fig. 8).[90] Within weeks of publishing the *Handbook*, the RSN was selling the 'new Tussah silks' at 8d per skein.[91]

Chapter 2 of the manual contains a comprehensive list of fabric grounds, ranging from linens, satins and silks to cottons, woollens and gold and silver cloth, though the great expense of the latter prevented their general use among amateur needlewomen. The *Handbook* offers advice on which textiles are suitable for furnishings (flax, Utrecht velvet, satin de chine, among others) and those that are suitable for clothing such as Kirriemuir twill used for tennis aprons and dresses. The manual also gives guidance on the materials that may be worked in the hand (mainly linens) in contrast to those that should only be worked in a frame (satins and silks generally, and some cottons and woollens). The *Handbook* goes so far as to recommend backing certain fabric grounds such as Genoa or Lyons velvet with a cotton or linen lining 'if [they are] to sustain any mass of embroidery'.[92]

Many of the fabrics listed were available for purchase through the RSN. Since its foundation, the School had acquired materials from specialist suppliers across the country. Serges, for example, came from John Aldam Heaton, owner of the Beehive Mills in Bradford, 'the best manufacturer of these goods in England' and 'one of the [RSN's] most indispensable workers'. Linens were bought from the old Dublin firm of Walpole Bros, which had a London outlet on Pall Mall. The silk mercers Lewis & Allenby on New Conduit Street supplied the RSN with silks and velveteens. The School purchased satins and linings from the furniture maker and retailer Maple & Co on Tottenham Court Road.[93]

Miss Higgin, who was interested in Aesthetic dress, particularly admired the new range of tussur silks produced by Wardle & Co, which she found 'charming' for summer dresses as well as chair back covers and embroidered window blinds.[94] The increase in exports of cultivated silk from the Far East during the mid nineteenth century had threatened to undermine the financial stability of the European silk industry. At his 'Art Printing and Dyeing Works' in Leek, Staffordshire, Wardle began experimenting with Indian tussur silk. The raw material was available in abundance on the sub-continent, but was used only in its natural state, the business of dyeing the yarn having eluded Indian dyers. Through the scientific use of mordants, Wardle not only succeeded in dyeing but hand-block printing tussur silk with fast, natural dyes.[95] The RSN kept abreast of developments in the textile industry. Miss Higgin noted in the *Handbook*:

> Within the last year successful experiments have been made in dyeing these Indian silks in England. The exact shades which we admire so much in the old Oriental embroideries have been reproduced, with the additional advantage of being perfectly fast in colour.[96]

The RSN went to considerable lengths to replicate antique fabrics. The School recommended Bolton or workhouse sheeting, a coarse, heavy twilled cotton fabric that resembled the twilled cotton 'on which so much of the old crewel embroidery was worked in the seventeenth century', for use on curtains, counterpanes, chair coverings and even ladies' clothing.[97] Russian crash, a coarse homespun linen, became a favourite of the crewel work room at the RSN because of the 'beauty of its tone of colour', but as the *Handbook* noted, 'though sent over in large bales, it is very difficult to find two pieces among a hundred that in any way match each other'.[98]

Stitches

The *Handbook* includes instructions for working over twenty different stitches found in crewel, silk and gold work, divided between those that are suitable for hand embroidery (stem, split, satin, blanket, French knot, bullion knot, chain, twisted chain or rope stitch and feather or long and short) and those that are best done in a frame. The latter are divided into four groups: couching or laid embroidery (plain couching, underside couching, net-patterned couching, brick stitch, diaper couching and basket stitch); cushion stitches (tent, simple cross, Persian cross and Burden stitch); cut work or inlaid and onlaid appliqué; and a miscellaneous group, comprising feather and stem, which according to the manual could be worked equally well in the hand or frame, as well as Japanese stitch (a variant on stem stitch) and tambour work.

Despite the editor's claim, not all the stitches described in the manual were in common use. Chain stitch, for example, had lost credibility among Victorian hand embroiderers because of the ease with which the sewing machine, first introduced into England in the early 1840s, could replicate the stitch.[99] The *Handbook* also contains a lengthy description of tambour work even though the technique had fallen into disuse in Britain and was not taught at the School during the 1870s.[100] Conversely, many other stitches found in crewel embroidery such as herringbone, 'used for filling in the foliage of large conventional floriated designs', are mentioned only in passing. According to Miss Higgin, 'Most of these, if required, can be shown as taught at the Royal School of Art Needlework, and are illustrated by samplers.'[101] In practice, most professional art embroiderers, including the RSN, used a small vocabulary of stitches – primarily long and short, stem, satin and French knot – when working contemporary designs, in the belief that 'Excellence of workmanship does not lie in many curious and difficult varieties of stitch, but in the expressive use of a few ordinary ones'.[102]

The method of working stitches presented in the *Handbook* conforms in the main to that taught today at the RSN,[103] though some of the terminology may seem foreign. For example, in the Victorian period, raised satin stitch worked over a padded foundation of running threads was known as 'French Plumetis'.[104]

Lady Alford, who was an admirer of the antiquarian Canon Daniel Rock,[105] was keen to restore the Medieval Latin terms for embroidery identified in Rock's 1870 catalogue of textile fabrics in the South Kensington Museum. Thus in the *Handbook* cushion stitches become *Opus Anglicanum* and feather stitch, the '[v]ulgarly called "*long and short stitch*"', is renamed *Opus Plumarium*, 'so called from its supposed resemblance to the plumage of a bird'.[106]

The section on cut work or appliqué contains advice on transferring antique textiles, the RSN having gained considerable experience in this area since its foundation.[107] The School had silks dyed specially to match the faded colours of the antique work so that without examining the back it was impossible to distinguish between the old and the new stitches where the School had cut out the embroidery and applied it to a new ground:

> Embroidery transferred in this manner is as good as it was in its first days, and in many cases is much better, for time often has the same mellowing and beautifying effect in embroideries as in paintings.[108]

Both chapters on stitching are peppered with specific examples of antique and modern needlework as well as general comments on the history of embroidery, added in all probability by Lady Alford, who was an authority on the subject. For instance, the instructions for working knotted stitch or French knot segue into a brief discussion on the stitch's use across cultures and centuries, including the Pekin knot found in Chinese embroidery from the Tang dynasty (618–907 AD) onwards and knotted stitches of varying sizes used to depict the foliage of trees and shrubs in seventeenth-century English raised work.[109] The chapter on cushion stitches refers to the interest in Cretan and Persian work 'of which so much has lately been in the market'. It welcomes the death knell for Berlin work, which Lady Alford blamed for the total collapse of decorative embroidery in late Georgian and early Victorian Britain, but predicts that the stitch 'will doubtless be revived again in some form after a time, as being well fitted for covering furniture on account of its firmness and durability'.[110] By the early 1910s, the RSN witnessed the decline in fashion for surface stitching in favour of *gros* and *petit point*, which became the mainstay of the crewel work room.

A few of the objects described in the *Handbook* belonged to the South Kensington Museum:

...which, seen by the light of Dr Rock's invaluable "Catalogue of Textile Fabrics" is an education in itself, of which the ethnological as well as the artistic interest cannot be over-estimated, and it is within the reach of all who can find time to bestow on it.[111]

The specimen of 'fine and beautiful diapering in gold [that] could scarcely be surpassed', referred to in the section on couching, can be identified as the banner stitched in coloured silks and gold on a white silk ground designed by the church architect and decorator, William Curtis Brangwyn (Victoria and Albert Museum no. 689–1868). Brangwyn, a follower of Pugin, had established a workshop in Bruges around 1865 that specialised in textiles.[112] Decorated with a symbolic representation of the Holy Sacrament, the banner was awarded the prize for embroidery from the Roman Catholic Congress of Malines in 1866 and a silver medal at the *Exposition Universelle de Paris* the following year. It was acquired by the South Kensington Museum in 1868 (Fig. 9).

Among the examples of cushion stitch cited in chapter 5 of the *Handbook* is 'a toilet cover of ancient Spanish work' (Victoria and Albert Museum no. 267–1880), which the Museum bought shortly before the publication of the manual. Made as a dressing table cover some time during the eighteenth century, the stylised design of flowers and birds is worked entirely of cushion stitches in black floss silk upon a linen ground.[113]

The chapter closes with a brief description of *Opus Anglicum* or *Anglicanum*, regarded by many textile historians as 'one of England's greatest cultural achievements', though the *Handbook* notes, 'it is strictly ecclesiastical, and therefore does not enter into our province'.[114] The sole aim of the RSN was to produce needlework 'for house decoration'.[115] Lady Welby never intended to compete with the Anglican and Roman Catholic convents or the firms of decorators that specialised in church work, a view reiterated in the preface to the manual.[116] However, in less than a decade, in May 1881, the RSN did introduce ecclesiastical embroidery to the work rooms, primarily to generate much-needed income.[117] Lady Alford based her comments on *Opus Anglicanum* on the research of Canon Rock. The *Handbook* refers specifically to the technique of working flesh that distinguished the English school of embroidery from German or Italian work of the thirteenth and fourteenth centuries, citing as a perfect example the Syon cope (Victoria and Albert Museum no. 83–1864), acquired by the South Kensington Museum in 1864 (Fig. 10).[118]

Contemporary readers of the *Handbook* would have recognised some of the antique examples from the School's Exhibition of Ancient Needlework, which opened in May 1878.[119] Among the specimens mentioned in the manual are:

1. An altar hanging worked entirely in basket stitch in gold on white satin belonging to a member of the RSN Managing Committee, Lady Alford's daughter-in-law, Adelaide, Countess Brownlow;[120]
2. A set of sixteenth-century Venetian curtains containing couched or laid embroidery, transferred and copied for Louisa, Lady Ashburton, a close friend of Lady Alford;[121]
3. A quilt couched with silks, described as 'a marvel of colouring and workmanship', exhibited by Mrs Alfred Morrison, a collector of European and Oriental antique embroideries who had served on the RSN Council;[122]
4. An Italian seventeenth-century wall hanging, the background worked in cushion stitch, lent by John, 5th Earl Spencer (his wife, Lady Charlotte Spencer, was elected to the RSN Council and sat on the Managing Committee);[123] and
5. A portrait of St Ignatius Loyola, probably of French origin, 'entirely executed in knots of such fineness, that without a magnifying glass it was impossible to discover the stitches'.[124]

The *Handbook* also contains references to embroideries made by the RSN including a bed hanging designed by William Morris for Mrs Wyndham,[125] and two objects sent to the Philadelphia International Centennial Exhibition in 1876. One was a replica of an antique counterpane belonging to Lady Brownlow that could still be seen in the School showroom in 1880. The other was Walter Crane's *Design for Decorating a Room with Hangings*, in which the figures were partially worked in Burden stitch, a variety of cushion stitch named after Morris's sister-in-law, Bessie Burden, appointed chief instructress of the RSN in July 1875.[126]

Framing

The embroidery frame described in chapter 4 of the needlework manual and the method of attaching the fabric to the bars are principally the same as that employed today at the RSN, except that the School now uses acid-free tissue instead of silver paper and wadding to prevent rolled up material from being marked (Fig. 11).[127] During the last quarter of the nineteenth century, the RSN preferred a free-standing frame, which liberated the stitcher's hands and gave access to the back of the embroidery, though these were cumbersome and expensive. For larger pieces of work, the School used wooden trestles that enabled the heavy frames to be raised or lowered at will (Fig. 12).[128] The manual also refers to the invention of a new frame sold by the RSN, which held the fabric ground in place by hinges attached to the bars rather than sewn to the webbing, creating tension by rolling the fabric round the bar.[129]

Finishing, Stretching and Cleaning

The *Handbook* closes with some useful advice for the modern embroiderer on stretching, finishing and cleaning needlework, though plunging one's hard-wrought crewel work into 'a lather made by water in which bran has been boiled' in order to clean 'without injury' is not for the faint hearted.[130] A variant on this method found in contemporary manuals was washing with gin and soft soap in the proportions of a quarter pound of soap to a half pint of gin if the work was particularly soiled.[131] Alternatively, the *Handbook* recommends using benzoline applied with a piece of clean flannel. Dry-cleaning solvent had been introduced into Britain in the late 1860s by the Scottish firm, John Pullar & Son of Perth, noted in the *Handbook* for their success in cleaning 'all kinds of embroidery without injuring it'.[132]

Needlework paste was commonly used during the Victorian period to anchor loose threads on the reverse of the work and to strengthen and stiffen embroidery destined to be mounted in screen panels and other items of furniture.[133] The RSN was not wholly in favour of the practice even in the 1870s, though the School recognised that in some cases 'it serves to steady the work…and make it wear better'.[134] The preferred method was shoemaker's paste, 'which is sure to bind, and will never come through on the surface of the material'.[135] The *Handbook* also recommends a recipe, 'said to be excellent', for embroidery paste made from flour, resin and water, devised by Mrs Dolby and revised by Lady Welby, that includes adding a teaspoonful of cloves in order to preserve the paste for up to six months.[136]

DESIGNS FOR EMBROIDERY

In its review of the *Handbook*, *The Queen* thought the designs particularly interesting as 'the greater part of them [had] been executed at various times by the ladies of the Royal School, and exhibited there.'[137] The Appendix was primarily a showcase for some of the RSN's best designs created by a group of artists whose connection with the School was familiar to every visitor who attended the needlework displays at Exhibition Road. *The Graphic* regarded many of the illustrations as 'really beautiful examples of artistic design'.[138]

The RSN had not always enjoyed such critical acclaim. In April 1874, the School had embarked on an ambitious display of work at the London International Exhibition of Art and Industry held at the South Kensington Museum. The exhibits received a mixed response from the press. 'Technicalities easily mastered, however complicated, are nothing', wrote *The Queen*, 'design is everything, and in this respect the exhibits on view, with a few exceptions, fail.' Faced with such '[a]n incongruous motley of indigested decorative ideas', the reviewer recommended that the RSN drop originality and consult the art relics of the past instead.[139]

In the wake of this criticism, the School immediately sought the advice of a number of experts and collectors in matters of art and design. Those consulted included the virtuoso Sir William Stirling-Maxwell, trustee of the British Museum and the National Gallery; the architect and designer George Aitchison; Edward Poynter, the first Slade professor at University College London; and the decorative artist John Hungerford Pollen, assistant keeper of the South Kensington Museum.[140] Pollen was engaged as director of the RSN in July 1874. He agreed to visit the School three or four times a week 'to superintend and pass designs and to give general assistance in matters of art',[141] but before the end of the year he had resigned because of his continued absence from the post.

Anxious to improve the RSN's design portfolio, Princess Helena persuaded the Council on 23 March 1875 to set aside a special fund for the purchase of designs from eminent artists. At the same meeting, the members agreed to form an advisory committee of gentlemen skilled in decorative work. Seven names were put forward and approved: Aitchison and Pollen; the artists Frederic Leighton, Edward Burne-Jones and Lawrence Alma-Tadema; and the architects William Burges and George Frederick Bodley.[142] On 12 May,

Mrs Wyndham met with Princess Helena and Lady Alford to discuss the formation of a 'permanent Art Committee' that would convene once a month to oversee the artistic direction of the School.[143] Leighton, Bodley and the artist Val Prinsep were invited to form such a committee. At their first meeting on 3 June 1875, the triumvirate recommended that in view of the RSN's desire to form a contemporary school of art needlework it should commission certain artists, including Burne-Jones, Aitchison, Morris and Crane, to submit designs.[144]

The RSN received an invitation to participate in the International Exhibition of Arts, Manufactures and Products of the Soil and Mine, staged in Philadelphia in 1876 to showcase America's industrial and cultural progress in the 100 years since the signing of the Declaration of Independence.[145] The fair played host to thirty-seven nations, from across four continents. The RSN display was one of the largest ever mounted by the School, for which it received a Certificate of Award, and in the opinion of the American interior designer, Candace Wheeler, 'sowed the seed' for the development of art needlework in the US.[146] In its preview of the specimens prepared for the Philadelphia exhibition, *The Queen* praised the Art Committee and its body of eminent designers, commenting:

> The school has gone through many phases and undergone many struggles until it achieved its present state of excellency, both as regards design and the artistic choice of colours; and if on former occasions we had to pass adverse judgment on the works of the Sloane-street establishment, we now cannot withhold our admiration of the high aims and able management of this most valuable institution.[147]

The newspaper also observed a 'marked improvement in [the] taste, style and technical skill' of the lady designers at the RSN, singling out the embroideries of Christiana Cresswell (Fig. 13)[148] and Rose Phillips, superintendent of the paint room, 'another artist of the needle, who promises to become a clever designer'.[149] The British and American press praised Mary Gemmell's talent for designing flowers in crewel work. *The Atlantic Monthly* commented:

> After the Japanese collection everything looks in a measure commonplace, almost vulgar. The English embroidery... in imitation of their models [is] either pitiably weak or like feverish fancies, quite disordered and

unnatural. The only piece of needlework we saw which held its own against Japan was a three-leaved screen by a Miss Gemmel (*sic*) of the Royal School of Art Needlework.[150]

A three-fold oriental style screen by the same designer received special mention in Walter Smith's retrospective account of the exhibition, *Examples of Household Taste* (Fig. 14):

> The amount of labor expended in design must have been very great, as in parts of it…the shading and gradations of color require minute stitches… It is an admirable example of the progress made by the institution in the brief time of its existence, in instructing women in the art of design and artistic needle-work.[151]

By 1880, the RSN studio or paint room employed around eighteen young female artists, some of whom were pupils at the National Art Training School, South Kensington, where Edward Poynter, the director and principal, had specially formed a class for them.[152] Here they were given a three-year training in free-hand drawing, water and oil painting, designing, and so on.[153] Promising students entered the RSN where they received further instruction before being admitted workers. Drawing pupils not enrolled at South Kensington did attend the art school once a week to hear a lecture and to study there for the rest of the day.[154]

The *Handbook* contains twenty-five specimens of embroidery designed by seven of the leading artists of the mid-Victorian period – Burne-Jones, Crane, Aitchison, Morris, Selwyn Image, Gertrude Jekyll and Fairfax Wade – and by three women from the RSN studio: Agnes Webster, Helen Burnside and Mary Herbert. The specimens are discussed in detail in Appendix I.

RSN BROCHURE

The final section of the *Handbook* contains an amalgam of leaflets printed by the RSN during the mid to late 1870s that sheds light on the organisation of the institution and its role in the development of art needlework in Britain at this time. The brochure comprises a prospectus for the RSN with a brief synopsis of the School's governance (pp [97]–99), details of classes available for amateur needlewomen in ornamental embroidery (p. [104]) and a price list of finished and prepared work, including a list of available designs, sold through the RSN and its provincial agencies (pp [100]–103, 105–106), details of which are discussed below.

Governance of the RSN

In setting up the RSN, Lady Welby hoped to make sufficient money to pay both the workers and the administrative staff a living wage and to defray expenses. It was never her intention that the School should make a profit. However, with the rate of expenditure habitually exceeding income from the sale and repair of embroidery, the RSN was soon dependent on donations and private money loans to carry out its operations. In March 1873, for example, the Duke of Northumberland, who was happy to assist 'a most deserving and suffering class of persons', lent the School £500 towards the purchase of materials. When it became clear that the loan could not be repaid, his wife informed Lady Welby that she would be happy to accept a bed quilt in lieu of the money as an advertisement of the RSN's skill and education in art; the proviso was that the School used materials in stock and the embroidery was only to be worked when the staff had nothing else to do.[155]

The RSN's precarious financial state was further exacerbated by the heavy losses incurred at the Philadelphia Centennial International Exhibition, which resulted in the resignation of several Council members and workers during the summer of 1877. In an effort to establish the School on a permanent basis, the RSN was incorporated on 1st April 1878 as a non profit-making limited company with an authorised share capital of £10,000. The Council hoped to raise a further £10,000 through the sale of debentures. It is unlikely that either sum was fully subscribed.[156]

The changing fortunes of the RSN are reflected in the governance of the School during the course of the 1870s. Initially Lady Welby and her husband had managed the RSN with the support of a council that comprised, for the most part, ladies from the upper echelons of English society who shared the principles on which the institution was founded. The increase in costs brought about by the move to Exhibition Road in June 1875 coupled with the need to run the RSN on a more business-like footing resulted in the formation of the Managing and Finance Committees, the respective powers of which were ratified in the 1878 *Memorandum and Articles of Association of the Royal School of Art Needlework*. The Managing Committee was responsible for overseeing the running of the RSN and had the power to appoint, employ and dismiss workers, teachers and administrative staff. It also determined levels of remuneration, devised rules and regulations for the internal management of the School, appointed agents to act on behalf of the RSN and set up a consultative body of artists to give advice on matters of taste,[157] but it had no power to authorise or incur expenditure without the consent of the Finance Committee. By 1880, membership of both committees was diverse and included patrons and collectors, some of whom had gallery and museum experience (Mrs Wyndham, Lady Charlotte Schreiber, Sir Coutts Lindsay and Edmund Oldfield), as well as prominent philanthropists (the Duke of Westminster and Mrs Stuart Wortley) and financiers and politicians (Sir William Gregory, Michael Biddulph and Lord Sudeley).[158] Brief biographies of the membership can be found in Appendix II.

Lessons

The brochure printed in the *Handbook* includes a variety of classes in ornamental needlework for amateur embroiderers held at the RSN's premises on Exhibition Road.[159] Frances Wells, who joined the School at its inception, had first raised the issue of giving lessons in October 1873 when she had been approached by a private lady who wished to stitch for her own drawing room.[160] Lady Welby was very reluctant to grant permission until such times as she might persuade the Council to introduce lessons for amateurs, fearing that Miss Wells might be strongly tempted to imitate some of the RSN's designs and to pass on the closely guarded knowledge she had learned. The staff was immediately informed that any worker who taught without the authority of the governing body stood to forfeit her connection with the School.[161]

At a meeting held at Alford House on 24 February 1874, the Council discussed a proposal for giving lessons in embroidery. Lady Welby assured its members that there was sufficient staff to carry out the scheme. Tuition would be provided initially in the pupil's home at the rate of 10s per hour, excluding expenses.[162] The proposal was carried unanimously and within a couple of months the RSN was giving lessons to a number of ladies approved by the Council.[163] The fee was reviewed in July of that year; an extra 5s per person was charged for two or more ladies wishing to receive a lesson during the same hour and an extra payment of 2s 6d made for each additional quarter of an hour.[164]

Following the re-organisation of the RSN in the summer of 1877, the Managing Committee proposed that a short instruction in needlework be offered at the School's premises on Exhibition Road, commencing on 16 October.[165] A flyer was printed outlining the course details comprising six one-hour lessons designed to teach ladies and children in 'every kind of stitch in Crewel, Silk and Gold'. The charges reflected the level of technical ability required for each type of needlework. Classes in crewel, silk and appliqué, and ecclesiastical embroidery cost £1 4s, £1 10s and £2 respectively, with an additional charge of 12s, 15s and £1 for two pupils or £1 4s, £1 10s and £3 for three pupils from a single family.[166] The flyer was reissued exactly one year later, offering the same range of lessons at exactly the same prices, but also included individual lessons of one hour at a rate of 7s on a lesson day, 8s 6d on a special day, the nature of which is not specified, and 10s 6d for ecclesiastical work at any time.[167] The cost of private lessons given in a pupil's home had risen since the 1874 rate to 10s 6d per hour plus expenses.[168] The September 1878 flyer was reprinted in the *Handbook* with the additional note that special terms were available for classes of twelve and upwards.

None of the records prior to 1880 discusses the manner in which the lessons were conducted. However, a flyer dating from February of that year, containing 'Instructions for Teachers' taking classes in provincial towns, gives some idea of the work done and the extra expenses involved:

Each pupil will be provided with a small piece of Linen, on which portions of various designs illustrating the different stitches will be drawn[.] For these and for the Crewels used during the Lessons, no charge will be made; but they will be retained by the Teacher – being the property of the School./ Samplers of Linen, containing varieties of Stitches will be supplied, if desired by the Pupil, with the Crewels for working, at a charge of 4/ or 5/, according to size and number of Sprays on each. These are, of course, the Pupil's own property, and may be taken home between the Lessons for Practice, and retained at the end of the Course./ The teacher will also take with her some pieces of prepared and commenced work, such as Cushions, Chairback Covers, or Footstools, so the Pupils may, if they choose, purchase the work and take their Lessons on it. Samplers for Silk Lessons will be 6/ or 7/, according to size.[169]

R S N   B r a n c h   S c h o o l

Amateur classes in ornamental needlework were also available at the newly formed Glasgow branch of the RSN.[170] Princess Helena first raised the issue of establishing branch schools or societies of affiliated workers in the country at a meeting of the Council in February 1875.[171] The following month the RSN received a letter from the amateur embroiderer Margaret Lowthian Bell, wife of the northern industrialist Sir Isaac Lowthian Bell, as regards the setting up of a school in Newcastle, though nothing seems to have come of the proposal.[172] Nearly two years later, *The Queen* announced the opening of a branch of the RSN, run along similar lines to the parent school, at the Queen's Institute, Dublin, the first technical college for women in Europe, under the patronage of Princess Helena and Louisa, Duchess of Abercorn, President and Vice-President respectively.[173] Apart from a reference to a letter sent by the secretary, Mrs Hely Hutchinson, a week before the opening on 5 February 1877, the extant records at the RSN make no mention of the Irish branch school, though the institution did display some of its work a month later at an exhibition of ancient and modern embroidery held in Dublin.[174]

'Anxious to extend to Scotland the advantages of an industry for gentlewomen so eminently suited to their capacities and tastes', the house furnishers Alexander & Howell submitted a proposal to the Managing Committee in April 1879 regarding the creation of a RSN branch school in Glasgow.[175] Not surprisingly, the firm's offer to pay all the expenses, to defray any possible losses and to divide the profits equally with the School, met with a favourable response.[176] A sub-committee made up of Princess Helena, Lady Alford, Lady Welby, and others was formed to discuss the logistics. At its meeting on 1st July the members resolved to send Miss Higgin to Scotland to ascertain the terms under which the school would be established, in particular whether the Glasgow branch would sell needlework or restrict itself to teaching. The sub-committee also stipulated that only designs produced by the parent school were allowed and that the local committee should be responsible only for the financial and not the artistic management of the branch school.[177]

Over the next few weeks, a contract was agreed with the guarantors, and the establishment of the Glasgow school was announced in the national press. *The Scotsman* printed a notice inviting ladies wishing to become workers in the school to apply to the secretary and advertised classes in ornamental needlework commencing on 6 October at the RSN's work rooms at 116 St Vincent Street, a few doors away from the School's show rooms at Alexander & Howell, right in the heart of the city.[178] Towards the end of the following year the *Glasgow Herald* announced, 'Some of the art products of this branch have been very favourably noticed in publications devoted to ladies' work for substantiality of texture and beauty of design'.[179] Despite its success, the Glasgow branch, along with the showroom opened in Edinburgh in November 1880 at 4 South Charlotte Street, were casualties of the financial difficulties that beset the RSN during the early 1880s and were forced to close in July 1884.[180]

Prepared and Finished Work

In view of the widespread craze for art embroidery during the 1870s, the introduction of prepared work for amateur needlewomen was a logical step for the RSN to take (Fig. 15).[181] The idea was first mooted at a Council meeting on 24 February 1874. Lady Welby reported:

> Now that we can venture to undertake it I am very anxious that it should be decided and generally made known that the School will now "prepare and begin" work for ladies to do, as tradesmen whose opinion can be trusted tell us that in Church-work Shops that department is so extremely remunerative that it pays for the others.[182]

Nine months later the manageress, Miss Wade, recommended the formation of a separate prepared work department with its own set of accounts.[183] The suggestion was adopted and the decision taken to find a suitable person who could be entrusted with the care of the department.[184] Alice Haworth (b. 1851), sister to the RSN secretary, became superintendent in 1875.[185]

The RSN supplied prepared work with the design traced on the fabric ground, a portion of the embroidery commenced and sufficient threads to complete the piece.[186] The School was also willing to trace and prepare materials provided by its customers, but requested that dresses, for example, should be cut out and tacked in advance and lines marked on the material to show where the design was to be placed. Prior to 1881, designs on paper were not available from the RSN under any circumstances. All designs supplied in the form of prepared work were the copyright of the School and could not be used for purposes of sale. The work was stamped with the VR/RSAN monogram and the letters 'PW' ('Prepared Work').

In 1878, the RSN issued flyers advertising prepared and finished work, copies of which were printed in the *Handbook*.[187] The School offered a range of soft furnishings in a variety of botanical and conventional designs,[188] including table, chair and sofa back covers, cushions, chair seats, curtains, table and curtain borders, piano panels, banner, table and folding screens, mantel valances and washstand backs. Bedding ranged from counterpanes and blankets to *berceaunette* covers. Clothing encompassed dress borders, children's dresses and aprons, opera cloaks, tennis aprons, fans and Algerian hoods. A variety of knickknacks included envelope boxes, photograph frames, tea cosies, bellows and knitting pockets (Fig. 16).

The prepared and finished work advertised in the *Handbook* was sold through the RSN showroom and its network of agents. Lady Welby reported to the Council on 24 February 1874 that some of the 'great Firms' were keen to procure art embroidery and were endeavouring to import workers from Paris. Anxious to avoid any danger of rivalry, she invited some of the 'most distinguished and powerful Houses' to send in formal applications 'for the honour of connection with the School'. The art furniture maker Henry Capel, who had been the sole trade agent since the RSN had opened in November 1872, was in favour of the proposal and offered to assist in any way he could.[189] Several letters from unspecified firms of interior decorators were read out at the Council meeting and their applications accepted.[190] By the end of the year the School had acquired at least nine additional London agents, including Maple & Co, the furniture maker and retailer on Tottenham Court Road, and the Garrett sisters, Agnes and Rhoda, who were among the best-known women designers and decorators of the period.[191]

By 1878, however, the RSN had dispensed with London agents, controlling sales in the capital directly from its premises on Exhibition Road, but the School retained and expanded its string of provincial agencies thus ensuring coverage nationwide.[192] The *Handbook* lists six outlets in major cities across the country: in East Anglia, the firm of cabinet makers and general furnishers Robertson & Sons of Norwich; in the Midlands, the cabinet makers Manton, Sons & Gilbert of Birmingham; in the North, the furniture makers Rumney & Love of Liverpool, E Goodall & Co of Manchester and Marsh, Jones and Cribbs of Leeds; and in Scotland, the house furnishers Alexander & Howell of Glasgow. The RSN also had an American agency situated in Boston, namely the carpet manufacturer Torrey, Bright and Capen.[193]

The School issued a flyer around 1878 setting out the terms and conditions for agents. Every article supplied by the RSN bore a stamped or embroidered trademark as well as a printed ticket stating that it was worked or prepared by the School. Agents were instructed not to remove, deface or conceal either the trademark or the ticket. Embroidered articles made by someone other than the RSN had to be kept separate and labelled accordingly. Agents were forbidden to 'copy or imitate or permit to be copied or imitated' any design produced by the RSN. In return, the School gave up to 12½% discount depending on the size and value of the order.[194]

PROPOSED SECOND EDITION

Sales of the *Handbook* were so successful that a second edition became necessary. Lady Alford agreed at a meeting of the Managing Committee on 19 May 1881 to undertake the task and arranged her own terms with Sampson Low & Co for the publication of the book, but as the Council was soon to discover, the situation was far from plain sailing.[195] Having revised the text, including re-writing the chapters on stitches, Lady Alford proposed dropping the words 'By Miss Higgin', which had been printed without her consent on the title page of the first edition.[196] The preface would contain a note recognising the assistance she had received from Miss Higgin and other ladies, in particular Mrs Bayman, superintendent of the work rooms.[197] Initially Miss Higgin asked that any reference to her be omitted from the preface, though Lady Alford felt that she 'deserved thanks for having laid the groundwork of the book'. However, on exploring the matter further, Miss Higgin was advised by her solicitors, Hudson & Co, that she was entitled to the copyright of the *Handbook*.

Unaware of this new development, Lady Alford signed a contract in her own name with Sampson Low & Co on 7 June 1882. This time she offered to pay all the expenses of the second edition, the publisher taking only a commission. At her request, Sampson Low & Co entered Lady Alford's name on the registration of the copyright at Stationers' Hall on 1st August 1882, having unwittingly failed to do so following the publication of the first edition.[198] However, less than two weeks later Miss Higgin entered her own name at Stationers' Hall as proprietor of the copyright in the *Handbook*.[199] In view of both claims, the Managing Committee felt it a matter of urgency to establish who owned the copyright: Miss Higgin, Lady Alford or the RSN. Lady Alford's solicitors, Nicholl Manisty & Co, suggested having their client's name removed instantly from the register while the question was decided, but were informed by the publisher that this could not be done without a judge's order. The case was therefore referred to Counsel.[200]

The dispute caused considerable disquiet among the members of the Managing Committee. Mary Wyndham, for example, recorded in her diary on 3 August 1882 that 'Mamma [was] full of this business between Lady Marian & Miss Higgin'. Towards the end of the month, Mrs Wyndham discussed the affair with her close friend Blanche, Countess of Airlie 'till 3 o'clock forgetting the time'. By the early autumn, the Wyndham household referred disparagingly to the author of the *Handbook* as 'Dame Higgin'.[201]

On 25 August 1882, Montagu Muir Mackenzie of 3 Temple Gardens delivered his opinion on the three core points outlined in the case sent to Counsel. As regards the first question – 'In whom is the copyright of the Handbook?' – Mackenzie ruled that Miss Higgin would have retained the copyright if her original manuscript had been published with the minimum of alteration. However, several persons had contributed to the final version of the *Handbook*, including Miss Herbert and Miss Stuart Wortley, who had prepared the majority of the illustrations. Cundall had carried out the arrangements for the publication and Lady Alford had edited the manuscript, and altered and added to the letterpress at proof stage. Having therefore failed to register her name as the proprietor of the copyright at the time of publication, Miss Higgin's claim was now untenable. The copyright was in the RSN and the right to republish the *Handbook* rested in the Managing Committee.

In answer to the second question – 'If it belongs to Miss Higgin, could she claim anything except the property of the original MSS, as written by her, without the alterations by Lady Marian, or, at all events, without the illustrations, plates, &c?' – Mackenzie was of the opinion that Miss Higgin had not retained her copyright either in the original manuscript that she submitted to the Managing Committee in March 1879 or in the form in which the text was ultimately published. Miss Higgin's position at the RSN and her 'complete acquiescence and co-operation in the whole arrangement' was vital to the case. At most, she had the right to republish her own manuscript and to restrain its republication by anyone else in a separate form or the use of it for any purpose other than that of a second edition of the *Handbook*.

As to the final question – 'Can Lady Marian publish the new book as a second edition… without infringing the rights of any other person?' – Mackenzie judged that Lady Alford did not own the copyright in the *Handbook* as her own personal property. The original manuscript had been accepted by the Managing Committee and had been edited on their behalf by Lady Alford. Furthermore, the RSN and not she had paid the various contributors. Without the sanction of the School, Lady Alford was not at liberty to publish a new edition.[202]

In the light of Counsel opinion, the Managing Committee voted at a special meeting held on 25 October 1882 neither to undertake nor to authorise the publication of a second edition for the time being and instructed the RSN's solicitor, Arthur Curtis Hayward, to take the necessary steps to remove Lady Alford's name from the registration at Stationers' Hall. Thanks were given to Miss Higgin 'for the manner in which she had placed herself unreservedly' in the hands of Princess Helena as regards the copyright.[203] At the meeting held three weeks later Lady Alford read out a letter from her own solicitors pointing out that Miss Higgin's name should also be removed at Stationers' Hall. Curtis Hayward was instructed to draw up an agreement between the three parties registering the copyright in the name of the RSN and to forward a copy of the submission to both sets of solicitors for approval. The Managing Committee also consented to Lady Alford's request for the return of a letter she had addressed to Miss Higgin shortly after signing the second contract with Sampson Low & Co.[204]

Curtis Hayward informed the Managing Committee on 19 January 1883 that the differences, which had arisen as to the copyright of the *Handbook*, might be amicably settled. A week later, Miss Higgin signed an indenture conveying 'all powers and authorities privileges profits and advantages' to the RSN. In the event of the School producing a new edition Miss Higgin's name would appear on the title page and no alteration would be made to the text without her consent.[205] A notice printed in *The Times* on 14 March 1883 (p. 5) stated that 'the name of the lady' entered under the Copyright Act had been removed. Curtis Hayward reported to the Managing Committee two days later that by order of the High Court of Justice Lady Alford's name had been withdrawn and the RSN registered at Stationers' Hall as the owner of the copyright.[206]

The following month the Managing Committee received letters from Lady Alford and Miss Higgin's solicitors requesting the RSN to pay their legal costs. The correspondence was referred to the Finance Committee, which reported on 24 May that after careful consideration it could not accede to their request.[207] The RSN was haemorrhaging money; the balance sheet at March 1883 showed debts of £1408, sales had fallen by £2097 and the loan from the bank amounted to £3000. Notwithstanding the limit in production, the value of stock in hand remained the same as the previous year, £12,424. In the absence of increased sales, the Duke of Westminster, head of the Finance Committee, recommended a reduction in staff by twenty-five workers with effect from 31 July, and warned 'should the Society be not in a more satisfactory position next year it may be impossible to continue working'.[208]

Lady Alford wrote to Princess Helena on 19 July 1883 resigning her post as Vice-President because she no longer felt able to face the responsibilities that she had accepted nearly twelve years previously, though in truth her decision to relinquish office was driven by the dispute over the *Handbook*. It was not until 15 November, after a lengthy summer recess, that the Managing Committee was informed of her resignation.[209] A second letter from Lady Alford, dated 13 November 1883, was read at that meeting in which she explained that fifteen months earlier she had at the suggestion of some members of the Finance Committee destroyed the second edition of the *Handbook* that she had 'revised and printed for the benefit and with the approval of' the RSN. In addition, she had written at their suggestion another book entitled *A New Guide to the Art of Embroidery*, probably the second part of the *Handbook* promised in the editor's preface to the first edition.[210] Keen that the RSN should maintain its position as the foremost instructor in art needlework, Lady Alford now offered the manuscript to the Managing Committee but with two provisos. First, a member of the committee would accept responsibility for seeing it through the press and secondly, that after paying the cost of publication the profits would go to the poor fund 'for the sick and suffering working members of the association'. In the event that the proposal was rejected, Lady Alford would publish the book on her own account and at her own discretion but would do nothing to hinder the action of the Committee. She also repeated a request made in August 1882 to examine the editor's copy of the first edition of the *Handbook*, which she believed was lodged with Miss Higgin's solicitor.[211]

The Managing Committee accepted with 'great regret' Lady Alford's resignation. They acknowledged the contribution she had made to the 'better cultivation of the art of ornamental needlework' and her efforts in promoting the interests of the workers. The members thanked her for 'her kind and public-spirited' offer to place at the RSN's disposal the manuscript of her new book on embroidery and referred the issue of publication along with her request to the Finance Committee for its consideration.[212] The latter resolved that the Managing Committee was not in a position to comply with Lady Alford's desire to see the editor's copy of the *Handbook* as this was not in the RSN's possession and instructed Miss Wade to enquire whether the School would be liable for the cost of publishing the new embroidery guide.[213] Following the recommendations made by the Finance Committee, the RSN rejected Lady Alford's offer on the grounds of the School's precarious financial state and the potential difficulty in revising the text prior to publication.[214] On 19 March 1884, she signed an agreement with Sampson Low & Co to publish her magnum opus, *Needlework as Art* (1886). In the preface, Lady Alford explained the relationship between this work and the earlier publication:

> In the Preface to the "Handbook of Art Needlework", which I edited for the Royal School at South Kensington in 1880, I undertook to write a second part, to be devoted to design, colour, and the common-sense modes of treating decorative art, as applied especially to embroidered hangings, furniture, dress, and the smaller objects of luxury./ Circumstances have since then, obliged me to reconsider this intention; and I have found it more practicable to cast the information which I have collected from Eastern and Western sources into the form of a separate work, which in no way supersedes or interferes with the technical instruction supposed to be conveyed in a handbook.[215]

The publication met with favourable reviews, *The Times* describing the volume as 'the best history of needlework that exists in English'.[216]

What of Miss Higgin? Aware of the RSN's need to make drastic cutbacks in spending, she offered to resign her secretarial post, worth £200 per annum, in June 1884.[217] The Managing Committee felt that her resignation would not prejudice the interests of the School and referred the offer to the Finance Committee for its opinion. In light of the recommendations laid by the Duke of Westminster before the Managing Committee on 7 July, 'best thanks' were given to Miss Higgin for her past services to the School. She would continue to receive her salary until 30 September, the date of her departure to be confirmed once the scheme for the re-organization and reduction in the number of staff was approved.[218] However, the RSN rejected her proposal to act as an agent on behalf of the School.[219]

Miss Higgin went on to carve out a successful career as the founder and manageress of The Society of Associated Artistes. The company specialised in embroidery applied to costume and by 1890 had become a first class West End business with no outstanding debts and a good clientele.[220] Miss Higgin also contributed needlework articles to a number of journals, including *The Art Journal* and the *Magazine of Art*, and penned a handbook entitled *Art as Applied to Dress* (Virtue & Co, London, 1885), which *The Scotsman* described as 'an earnest and thoughtful plea for the necessity of mastering and recognising aesthetic rules and principles in regard to dress'.[221] The 1901 census lists her occupation as 'Writer Novelist Author', having published at least four novels with a guidebook to Spain destined for the press the following year.[222]

North American Publications Derived from the RSN Handbook

Meanwhile, across the Atlantic two Bostonian publishers were printing extracts from the *Handbook*, in all probability without the knowledge of the RSN.[223] The vogue for art needlework had taken the city by storm. A school of embroidery, modelled on the RSN, was established at Boston's Museum of Fine Arts in 1878.[224] The RSN's sole American agent, Torrey, Bright and Capen, was based in the city, as was its successor, A H Davenport & Co, which supplied luxury furniture and interior decorations to the country's elite.[225] Drawing on English and American sources, the Bostonian publisher S W Tilton & Co issued numerous floral embroidery designs for mantelpiece borders, chair backs, banner screens, cushions, curtains, and so on, complete with instructions on drawing, tracing and transferring patterns and directions for stitching.[226] In 1879, the firm published *Art Needlework for Decorative Embroidery: A Guide to Embroidery in Crewels, Silks, Appliqué, etc*, edited by Lucretia Peabody Hale (1820–1900), Bostonian author and advocate of women's education. The second edition, printed two years later, contains 'Instructions given at the Royal School for Art-Needlework at South Kensington, England'. The first chapter, including the illustrations, was lifted verbatim from chapters 3 and 5 of the RSN needlework manual.[227] The American editor added a handful of notes, commenting, for example, that 'chain stitch is used less here as outline, because it can be so easily imitated by the machine that it does not gain the credit of being hand-work'. Hale refers the reader to successive numbers of 'Tilton's Art-Needlework Series' for the many varieties of stitches not explained in the *Handbook*.[228]

Within weeks of the publication of the RSN manual in January 1880, a second American publisher, Perry Mason & Co, printed an eight-page pamphlet entitled *Hand-book of Embroidery; Kensington Stitches Described and Illustrated. As Taught at the Royal School of Art-Needlework, at South Kensington, England*.[229] Priced at 10 cents, the booklet is a poorly edited distillation of the RSN chapter on embroidery worked in the hand. It omits the instructions for slip stitch, bullion knots, chain stitch and twisted chain or rope stitch as well as the illustration that accompanies the explanation on working blanket stitch. The publisher did not even bother to re-number the remaining stitch diagrams, taken directly from the RSN manual, so that 'no. 10' immediately follows 'no. 4' in the Boston edition. The *Hand-book* was reissued in 1883, this time with additional instructions for knotted stitch or French knot crammed onto the final two pages of the pamphlet (Fig. 17).

Despite the shortcomings of Perry Mason & Co's *Hand-book*, the Boston publications not merely complimented the RSN but illustrated the influence played by the School on the dissemination of art embroidery in the US during the last quarter of the nineteenth century. *The Atlantic Monthly*, for example, commented that the impulse that led to the formation of art needlework schools across the country 'was derived from South Kensington (England), and affords a striking instance of the ramifications of an organization.'[230]

* * * * * * *

Aymer Vallance in his 1897 review of the RSN praised the School's promoters '[who] may with justice claim to have led the van of a much-needed and very admirable reformation' in art embroidery. He believed that the key to the RSN's success lay in its thorough and systematic training in which 'the whole grammar of embroidery is taught from the very rudiments upwards', drawing particular attention to the *Handbook of Embroidery* and the contribution it had made to the literature of the art of the needle.[231] At the time of its publication, the manual received critical acclaim from the press, the *Daily News* describing it as 'an authoritative exposition of the mystery of art-needlework as practised by its most eminent professors'.[232] The *Handbook* underpinned the RSN's commitment to the technical training of women and their employment in the decorative arts. The collaboration between Miss Higgin and Lady Alford ensured that the volume was not only a technical guide to stitching but a commentary on the role played by the School in the rediscovery of antique needlework and the latest developments in textile manufacture. Moreover, the Appendix containing designs for embroidery was an inspired piece of marketing, demonstrating the RSN's close relationship with many of the leading figures in the Aesthetic and Arts and Crafts movements, a relationship that was to continue up to the First World War.

Lynn Hulse, April 2010

APPENDIX I

Designs For Embroidery

Edward Burne-Jones
Plate 1. *Design for a Wall Panel*
Date: 1875

Burne-Jones's earliest recorded design for embroidery dates from 1863. Based on Chaucer's poem *The Legend of Good Women*, the theme first appeared as a series of tiles designed for Morris, Marshall, Faulkner & Co in 1862. The following year the artist produced a running frieze on the same subject as a gift for his friend and mentor John Ruskin, to be stitched by the girls of Winnington Hall School in Cheshire, but as his wife Georgiana later recorded, 'the joint embroidery scheme proved impracticable and the drawings alone remained as a symbol of loving intentions'.[233] Burne-Jones returned to Chaucer's works for his next major embroidery project, *Romaunt of the Rose*. Designed over the period 1874–1876 for the dining room of Rounton Grange, home of the northern industrialist Sir Isaac Lowthian Bell, the seventy-foot long frieze, which explores many aspects of courtly and philosophical love, was the first of a number of collaborative textiles produced by Morris & Co with Burne-Jones supplying the figurative composition and Morris the background detail.[234]

On 26 October 1875 Princess Helena and Lady Alford visited Burne-Jones to see the design he had created for the RSN, which the Vice-President thought 'quite charming'.[235] Accepted by the Art Committee four weeks later, *Musica* was stitched under the direction of Miss Burden in the crewel work room specially created for contemporary designs. Early in March 1876 the wall panel was displayed briefly in 'the public room of the school' among the objects destined for the Philadelphia International Centennial Exhibition 'so that those interested in such matters may inspect them'. The *Pall Mall Gazette* proclaimed Burne-Jones's design 'the most refined piece of work' on show:

> The masterly drawing of the figures, the excellent balance of quantities
> in the composition, the modesty of the materials used, and the simplicity
> of the stitch, all combine to render this piece of needlework artistic in
> the highest sense. The groundwork is of pale brownish linen, and the

embroidery on it is of darker brown crewels. Apollo is represented playing his lyre and seated on a pedestal beneath outspreading fruit-trees. Below are females performing on cymbals and harps. We understand that this is the first work of its kind made at the school and in all respects it is successful.[236]

Yet, despite the fact that Burne-Jones is listed among the artists reputed to have furnished designs for the American fair, there is no mention of *Musica* in any of the articles printed in the British press during the weeklong preview exhibition (21–28 March) held in the RSN showroom.[237] The detailed coverage that later appeared in the US was equally silent as regards Burne-Jones's contribution to the Philadelphia display. The RSN may have withdrawn the panel shortly after the publication of the *Pall Mall Gazette* review.[238]

In March 1877, the School offered for sale the greater part of the specimens that had failed to find purchasers at Philadelphia along with some new works never before exhibited, including *Musica*. *The Queen* thought the panel 'well worthy of attention…the design is characterised by extreme grace and boldness. The execution of the embroidery is simply admirable'.[239] The *Magazine of Art* later described the panel as:

> …*sui generis* for the needle – at least the greater portion of it was; and it was only in regard to the reproduction in embroidery of certain delicate lines, for giving subtle expression to a face or drapery, that we might take exception.[240]

Musica was also included in a major exhibition of ancient, oriental and modern embroidery held in Glasgow in October 1879 to celebrate the opening of the RSN's first branch school in Scotland.[241] The design was printed the following year in the *Handbook* as an example of the style of needlework that is 'very suitable for internal decoration, where a good broad effect is required without a large amount of labour.'[242]

Burne-Jones's portière for a music room was copied several times, 'and will doubtless continue to be a favourite', noted an article published in the *Magazine of Art* to mark the tenth anniversary of the RSN in 1882.[243] The Duke of Westminster, for example, acquired around this time a solid, coloured version of *Musica* worked in crewels on a linen ground (Fig. 18). The panel, which is now in a private collection, differs from the design published in the *Handbook* and in the *Magazine of Art*. The honeysuckle border is absent and the figures stand on stone paving rather than on a carpet of flowers.[244]

Musica was conceived as one of a pair of hangings devoted to the sister arts. In the Burne-Jones collection of drawings at Birmingham Museums and Art Gallery there is a preliminary pencil sketch for *Poesis*.[245] Princess Alexandra, who became patron of the RSN in *c*1877, sent a version of *Poesis*, embroidered by the School in wool on cotton, to the Melbourne International Exhibition of 1880 to be sold for charity (Fig. 19). The hanging was later given to the city's National Gallery of Art.[246]

Mrs Wyndham owned cartoons of *Musica* and *Poesis*, enlarged by Burne-Jones's assistant, Charles Fairfax Murray, and completed by the artist himself in 1881 when staying at Clouds, the Wyndhams' Wiltshire residence. Mary Wyndham recorded in her diary on 23 April for that year that Burne-Jones had drawn a design 'for Mama to work', generally assumed to be *Poesis*. The cartoons were sold in the contents sale of Clouds in 1933; *Poesis* reappeared in a Sotheby's auction on 23 June 1981.[247]

During the early 1900s, Mrs Wyndham lent her original cartoons to the RSN to be copied into needlework. Lady Jane Cory (*c*1870–1946), wife of the colliery proprietor and oil refiner Sir Clifford Cory, who lived with her sister at 28 Belgrave Square close to the Wyndhams, borrowed the School's copy of *Musica* as a model for her own embroidery. In an interview that she gave in the 1906 Christmas issue of *Needlecraft*, Lady Cory described the panel, worked in crewels on a linen ground, as 'her favourite piece of work'. Taking seven and a half months to complete, it was her first figure subject. The composition of the panel is the same as the Duke of Westminster's version. Despite having 'a positive dislike to needlework of any description' in her childhood, she later had lessons in embroidery at the RSN, including 'five hours' special instruction in the art of working faces for my "Musica".'[248] Lady Cory completed *Poesis* in 1908 and the pair hung in adjacent recessed panels at Belgrave Square. Following her death in 1946, the National Art Gallery, Wellington, New Zealand, acquired *Musica* and *Poesis* along with seven other embroideries worked by Lady Cory.[249] A second pair, made by students from the RSN training school for Mrs Hornby Lewis, a Council member, was exhibited in the Grafton Galleries in January 1907; the present whereabouts is unknown.[250]

Walter Crane
Plate 2. *Design for a Wall Panel*
Date: 1875–1876
Plates 14–15. *Designs for Table Borders*
Date: 1875–1876

From the early 1870s, the illustrator and painter Walter Crane began to develop his career as a decorative artist, working in a variety of media, including wallpapers, mosaic, stained glass, plaster and gesso relief, ceramics, textiles and embroidery.[251] His earliest commission for the RSN, dating from July 1875, was the four-panel screen based on Aesop's fable *The Vain Jackdaw*, one of the most enduring designs produced by the School in the last quarter of the nineteenth century.[252] Over a period of about twenty years, the artist produced a variety of classical, grotesque and naturalistic patterns for the RSN. The design for a wall panel illustrated in Plate 2 of the *Handbook*, described by the *Pall Mall Gazette* as 'an original and very decorative arrangement of fruits, garlands of flowers, peacocks, monkeys, mermaids, &c', formed part of Crane's *Complete Design for Decorating a Room with Hangings*, the centrepiece of the RSN's display at the Philadelphia exhibition (Fig. 20).[253] This 'exquisite work of decorative art' comprised two large classical figures in oblong panels, or portières, stitched in coloured crewels on white sateen representing the Latin salutations 'Salve' and 'Vale'.[254] To the left and right of the portières hung two wall panels in the grotesque style, later known as the *Elements* (the design printed in the *Handbook*), worked on figured gold twill, and above on a valance sat the three fates, Clotho, Lachesis and Atrophos, spinning the thread of life. Immediately above hung a festoon and basket valance on which was embroidered the name of the School. A stripe and leaf dado on sateen, two pilasters on white sateen and a frieze depicting figures of the arts – music, poetry, architecture and drawing – framed the whole. The frieze was stitched on a green ground, above which were the words '*Ars longa, vita brevis*', the first two lines of a Latin translation of an aphorism by the ancient Greek physician Hippocrates, meaning 'art is long, life is short'.[255]

The composition of the design illustrated in the *Handbook* conforms exactly with the panel sent to Philadelphia. However, Crane produced variations on the *Elements* for a five-fold screen, a specimen panel of which was sent to the RSN exhibition of ancient, oriental and modern embroidery at Glasgow in 1879 along with the *Complete Design for Decorating a Room with Hangings*.[256] Among the artist's papers in the Kensington Central Library are two preparatory watercolour sketches, one of which is labelled 'Screen panel Lady M Alford R.S.A.N' (Fig. 21).[257] A five-fold screen incorporating three different versions of the *Elements* design in the arrangement A–B–C–B–A, stitched in wools on a satin ground with an inscription embroidered in ancient Greek taken from Theocritus, can be found in the Victoria and Albert Museum (Fig. 22).[258] A second pair of panels with a much-reduced version of the design, stitched in crewels on a satin ground, was probably embroidered at the RSN in the late 1870s (Fig. 23).

Despite the accolade that Crane received from the press in 1876,[259] *The Times* was less enthusiastic about the inclusion of the *Elements* design in the *Handbook*:

> Heterogeneous compositions for panels…in which mermaids, monkeys, satyrs, serpents, peacocks, pomegranates, snails, grapes, toads, and cornucopiæ are fantastically pressed into service for occult decorative purposes, are less desirable as examples for broad distribution in the interests of public instruction in design.[260]

The reviewer preferred instead floral and naturalistic patterns like Plates 14 and 15, Crane's *Daffodil* and *Primrose* table borders, describing them as 'generally effective and in good taste' (Fig. 24).[261] Stitched in solid embroidery in crewel or silk, the borders were first displayed at the Philadelphia Exhibition.[262]

George Aitchison

Plate 3. *Design for a Quilt or Table Cover*
Date: *c*1873
Plate 7. *Design for a Sofa-Back or Piano Panel*
Date: *c*1877

George Aitchison, who was a member of the Holland Park circle, was much in demand as an interior decorator during the mid-Victorian period.[263] Between 1869 and 1871, he redesigned parts of the interior of the Wyndhams' London residence at 44 Belgrave Square.[264] His earliest recorded pattern for embroidery, dating from 1873, was a white satin counterpane designed for Mrs Wyndham and worked by the RSN.[265] At a Council meeting held at the School on 28 April 1874, Aitchison was chosen as a referee for design. His name was also proposed the following year as a potential candidate for the Art Committee.[266]

The RSN formally invited Aitchison to submit designs in July 1875.[267] A portière in blue, red and gold with an elaborate floral border, drawn for the School in December of that year, is among the designer's papers at the Royal Institute of British Architects.[268] A portfolio in the RSN archive also contains two floral patterns that he submitted to the Art Committee in October 1876 (Fig. 25; cover illustration).[269] Plate 3 of the *Handbook*, a design for a quilt with a border and centre powdering of pomegranates and sunflowers, embroidered in crewels on a satin ground, is closely based on the pattern Aitchison had earlier created for Mrs Wyndham.[270] The *Handbook* also contains an hibiscus design for a sofa back cover or piano panel, worked in two shades of blue silk on hand-woven linen or satin de chine. This may correspond with the sofa-back pattern offered for sale at a cost of £7 at the Special Exhibition of Needlework in March 1877.[271]

Fairfax Blomfield Wade
Plate 4. *Designs for a Wall Panel or Curtain*
Date: before 1880
Plate 5. *Design for a Quilt or Couvre-Pied*
Date: *c*1875–1876
Plate 8. *Design for Appliqué*
Date: before 1880
Plate 13. *Design for a Table Border*
Date: before 1880

Several members of the Wade family are connected with the early history of the RSN. Arthur Fenwick Stevenson Wade (b. 1837) produced a number of designs for the School during the winter of 1873–1874.[272] Lady Welby was much taken with the artist, commenting 'his drawing shows great talent & feeling for quaintness & we will freely make use of him.'[273] Wade's sister Louisa (b. 1845) was appointed assistant manageress of the RSN in February 1874 and was promoted to manageress nine months later in place of Lady Welby, who had resigned on the grounds of ill health.[274] Three of Wade's younger sisters, Octavia, Edith and 'a young one who draws', were part of the 'band of amateur workers and helpers' enlisted to complete embroideries begun at the School or to assist with tracing and pricking.[275] As the offspring of Nugent Wade, Anglo-Catholic rector of St Anne Soho and Canon of Bristol, the sisters had no real need to work for a living, unlike most of the women employed in the work rooms.[276]

Wade's younger brother Fairfax (1851–1919) began his career as a clerk in the Bank of England, but soon followed Arthur's example. Articled to the architect Sir Arthur William Blomfield in September 1872, he set up his own commercial practice towards the end of 1875.[277] Wade is remembered today chiefly as the architect of the RSN's new premises on the corner of Imperial Institute Road and Exhibition Road (Fig. 26), opened in 1903, but he began by designing floral borders and seat covers for the School from around August 1874 (Fig. 27).[278] His designs displayed at the Philadelphia Exhibition merited the attention of the press on both sides of the Atlantic:

> It altogether strikes us that amongst all the professional designers associated with the school Mr Wade seems to have best succeeded in an unpretending way of blending modern taste and artistic requirements. [279]

Four of Wade's designs, including a quilt or *couvre-pied* with squares of Greek or *guipre* lace displayed at the Philadelphia exhibition, were printed in the *Handbook*. [280] Lady Emily Plowden (1841–1915), wife of the Indian civil servant and Liberal MP Sir William Chichele Plowden, is credited with the completed version of Wade's design for a wall panel or curtain (*Handbook*, Plate 4), now in the Victoria and Albert Museum. Stitched in silks in outline and solid, the panel contains a repeating pattern of peonies, violets and rose-like flowers (Fig. 28).[281]

William Morris
Plate 6. *Design for a Sofa-Back Cover*
Date: *c*1875–1876
Plates 19–20. *Two Designs for a Wall Hanging*
Date: *c*1875–1876

Following the recommendations of the Art Committee, William Morris visited the RSN in July 1875 where he had a 'long and favourable interview' with Mrs Wyndham, promising designs 'that could be proceeded with'.[282] Later that month Leighton invited Morris to form one of the committee of artists and asked him to submit designs to the School.[283]

Some of the embroideries that Morris created for the RSN won critical acclaim at the Philadelphia exhibition, in particular the peacock and vine dado, described as 'equal in conception to many of the works of the best masters of mediæval decorative art'.[284] The *Handbook* contains at least one of Morris's patterns sent to the American fair. May Morris bequeathed to the Victoria and Albert Museum a needlework design in her father's hand which corresponds with the sofa-back cover, worked in outline on hand-woven linen in two shades of gold-coloured silks, displayed at Philadelphia and subsequently printed in the *Handbook*.[285]

The design for the honeysuckle screen with a blue worked ground listed in the 1876 exhibition catalogue does not survive but there is good reason to believe that it matched the wall hanging illustrated in Plate 20 of the *Handbook*. If this was indeed the case, then *Honeysuckle* may have originated as an embroidery design made for the RSN, thus pre-dating Thomas Wardle's manufacture of the pattern as a printed cotton for Morris & Co towards the end of 1876.[286] May's older sister, Jenny, and their mother, Jane, embroidered a curtain or hanging in silks over an outline version of the printed fabric that was exhibited at the first Arts and Crafts Exhibition in 1888.[287] Both the needlework panel and the design plate printed in the *Handbook* omit the leafy ground found in the printed textile and in the original watercolour design preserved in the Birmingham Museums and Art Gallery's collection of prints and drawings.[288]

The wall hanging illustrated in Plate 19 may correspond with the embroidery stitched in outline on Bolton sheeting exhibited at Philadelphia.[289]

Gertude Jekyll

Plates 9–10. *Designs for Chair-Seats or Cushions: Periwinkle and Iris*
Date: *c*1874–1879

Gertrude Jekyll's association with the RSN dates back to the summer of 1872 when she and Mrs Wyndham met with Lady Welby to discuss the formation of a 'School of Art Needlework for distressed gentlewomen'.[290] In October of that year her name appeared on a prospectus announcing the opening of the RSN as one of the ladies 'wish[ing] to assist in restoring needlework for house decoration to the level of other decorative arts', though she never played an active role in the running of the School.[291] Jekyll had begun exhibiting embroideries based on her own designs at the Workmen's International Exhibition in 1870 and over the following decade, she received needlework commissions from a number of artists and collectors, including members of the Holland Park circle.[292] She supplied the RSN with a selection of designs for chair seats or cushions, including daisy, star, cornflower and jessamine, as well as periwinkle and iris published in the *Handbook*.[293] The following year, the American writer Constance Harrison printed Jekyll's periwinkle and iris patterns among her recommendations on drawing room chairs in *Woman's Handiwork in Modern Homes*, though she omitted to name the designer.[294]

Selwyn Image

Plates 17–18. *Designs for Wall Panels: Juno, Minerva, Venus and Proserpine*
Date: *c*1879

The Wades may have been responsible for introducing Selwyn Image to the RSN. Ordained in 1872, he served as curate at St Anne Soho (1877–1880) under the Reverend Nugent Wade. Image attributed his 'small power of design' to John Ruskin, with whom he had studied drawing at Oxford, and began exhibiting work during his curacy. Best known for his designs for stained glass, he worked in a variety of media.[295]

Image produced a number of embroidery designs for the RSN, beginning with a four-panel screen portraying the Roman goddesses *Juno, Minerva, Venus* and *Proserpine*. The design was first displayed in 1879 at the Glasgow exhibition of ancient, oriental and modern embroidery and was printed the following year in the *Handbook* as a set of wall panels.[296] The series of figures was so successful that several versions have survived, worked in solid and/or outline:[297]

1. A four-panel Aesthetic movement walnut screen embroidered in silks and wools on linen in a variety of stitches, Christie's sale of *Art Nouveau, Art Deco and Studio Pottery*, 3 March 1981, pp 46–47, lot no. 197; the present whereabouts is unknown.[298]

2. Three panels (*Juno, Minerva* and *Venus*), the figures and leaves worked in outline and the birds and flowers in solid silks, on a satin de chine ground, possibly from the original Glasgow exhibit, Christie's sale of *Quilts, Costumes and Textiles* on 16 April 1998, p. 30, lot no. 270.[299] *Juno* and *Minerva* were resold in June 2008 in Patch Rogers's *Arts and Crafts Selling Exhibition*, Liberty, Regent Street, London; private collection (Fig. 29).[300]

3. *Venus* panel worked in coloured floss and silks, described erroneously as 'a young female saint', Sotheby's sale of *Costumes and Textiles 1500–1960* on 24 September 1980, p. 41, lot no. 336; the present whereabouts is unknown.[301]

4. A large panel, measuring approximately 250cm high by 150cm wide, based on the design *Venus* with a trellis background and floral border, stitched in outline in brown crewel on a linen ground. Formerly in the possession of the rock star Jimmy Page, the panel was sold at Sotheby's in Paul Reeves's *The Best of British Design from the 19th and 20th Centuries*, 20 March 2008, lot no. 75; private collection (Fig. 30).

5. Four-panel screen worked in outline in brown crewel on a linen ground, RSN Textile 1350. The reverse contains four identical carnation panels, probably designed by Nellie Whichelo (1862–1959), who joined the RSN studio in 1879.[302] The frame is decorated with the same set of carvings found on the Gemmell screen sent to the Philadelphia exhibition.[303]

6. *Proserpine* panel worked in silks on a linen ground by Miss J H Jones of the RSN, dated *c*1890; the present whereabouts is unknown.[304]

7. A three-panel screen (*Juno, Venus* and *Proserpine*) worked in silks, dating from *c*1900; private collection.[305]

Designs from the RSN Studio

Plate 11. Miss Webster, *Design for a Border*

Date: 1879

Plate 12. Miss Burnside, *Design for a Curtain or Table Border*

Date: 1879

Plate 16. Mary Herbert, *Design for a Table Border*

Dare: 1878–1879

Born in King's Lynn, Norfolk in December 1856, Agnes Webster was the daughter of George Webster, a newspaper reporter and editor.[306] She had studied at the National Art Training School, South Kensington and was sent by Poynter to the RSN in 1879.[307] She left within a few months to study and practice wood engraving but continued to supply designs to the School following her marriage to the painter George Clausen in June 1881.[308] Miss Webster's printed border design of paired griffins stitched in outline in silk or crewel is the only identifiable example of her work in the RSN Archive.[309]

Helen Marion Burnside, who was born at Bromley, Middlesex in 1842, joined the RSN as a designer in or around 1879.[310] Two of her designs were exhibited at the opening of the RSN's branch school in Glasgow in October of that year, namely a three-panel screen embroidered in crewels in feather stitch on oatcake linen and another embroidered on 'smock' linen in crewels. The floral design printed in the *Handbook*, which also dates from 1879, was intended for a curtain or table border.[311] Preserved in the RSN Archive is an undated painting of a magnolia, attributed to the designer (Fig. 31).[312] Miss Burnside remained in the studio until July 1888 when she took up an appointment elsewhere but continued to supply designs to the School.[313]

In addition to the ornamental head and tailpieces dispersed throughout the *Handbook*, Mary Herbert's tiger lily border design, worked in outline or solid in crewel or silk embroidery, was printed in the Appendix.[314] In the winter of 1880–1881, Lady Hamilton-Gordon invited *Harper's Bazar* to view the work of the School,[315] and in January 1881, the American fashion newspaper published Miss Herbert's tiger lily pattern, the second in its series of RSN designs, along with detailed instructions on materials, colour and stitching:

> It is intended for valances, table-cloth borders, or anything requiring a long horizontal strip. As a band for curtains or portières, it is especially

suitable, and, done in natural size, is very striking. As is readily seen, it is a conventional tiger-lily – that is, drawn to give the general effect of the flower, without being an exact copy. Hence it is entirely permissible to work the pattern in other than the colors of nature./ The pattern is adapted both to crewel-work and to appliqué, and the choice of style should be determined by appropriateness to the article it is to decorate./ Let it be supposed, for instance, that a portière is to be wrought in applied-work. The body of the curtain is of dark brown cloth or flannel; the strip on which the embroidery goes is dull gold, finished at the edges with a band of plush of a dark, dull, yellowish-red, the lower plush band being twice the width of the upper one. The plush bands are caught down with fancy stitches with gold-colored silk. The design is done in velvet or plush, the leaves in two shades of olive brown, lighter than the body of the drapery, and the cup of the flower in a peculiar shade of yellowish-red, paler than the plush bands, and in hue something between Pompeiian red and preserved-quince color. The stamens and spots on the petals are to be worked in black embroidery silk, and the veins in the leaves in yellow. The edges of the leaves and flowers must, of course, be worked down in some kind of what is known as couching – that is, cord, twists of silk, or gold thread, laid over the raw edge of the figure. Couching outlines are made of thick strands of double crewel, double strands of filoselle, cord, and sometimes even of ribbon. They are laid exactly over the edge of the applied leaf or blossom, and are sewed down by single stitches crossing them at regular intervals, either at right angles or diagonally, according to the fancy of the worker… The tiger-lily worked in crewel embroidery – which has already been fully described – about half the size of nature, is a beautiful border for a table-cloth, either between bands of plush or without them. Olive green leaves, rose red petals with yellow coronas, and black spots and stamens, are a beautiful combination on a dark green or very deep red ground; but no combination is more decorative than the colors of nature on any ground that will bear the peculiar though superb red-yellow of the growing tiger-lily.[316]

Appliqué Designs
Plate 21. *Design for a Border for Appliqué from Ancient Italian Work*
Date: before 1880
Plate 22. *Italian Design Showing the Application of Transposed Appliqué*
Date: before 1880

Neither of the designs produced for the appliqué and gold work room can be
identified, though much of the decorative cut work stitched by the department
was based on antique textiles borrowed from Council members or displayed in
the 1873 and 1878 exhibitions of ancient needlework.[317]

Fig. 26 Royal School of Art Needlework, architect Fairfax B Wade, 1903.

APPENDIX II

Managing Committee Members, 1880
(listed alphabetically by surname)

Mrs Louisa Baring (née Bulteel) (1839–1892)
Daughter of John Crocker Bulteel; married the banker Edward Baring in 1861, head of the family firm Baring Bros & Co, director of the Bank of England (1879–1891) and later chairman of Lloyd's (1887–1892). Joined the RSN Council some time before March 1877.[318]

Georgina Berkeley (née Holme-Sumner), Baroness Fitzhardinge of Bristol (1831–1897)
Daughter of William Holme-Sumner; married Francis William Fitzhardinge Berkeley, 2nd Baron Fitzhardinge in 1857. Joined the RSN Council some time before April 1873.[319]

Adelaide Brownlow-Cust (née Chetwynd-Talbot), Countess Brownlow (1845–1917)
Daughter of Henry Chetwynd-Talbot, 18th Earl of Shrewsbury; married Adelbert Brownlow-Cust, 3rd Earl Brownlow (see below), second son of Lady Marian Alford in 1868. Member of the Managing Committee by April 1878.[320]

Katrine Cowper (née Compton), Countess Cowper (1845–1913)
Eldest daughter of William Compton, 4th Marquess of Northampton and niece of Lady Marian Alford; married Francis Thomas de Grey Cowper, 7th Earl Cowper in 1870. Vicereine of Ireland (1880–1882) and founder of the Royal Irish School of Art Needlework in 1882. Joined the RSN Council some time before March 1877.[321]

Cecilia Dawnay (née Molyneux), Viscountess Downe (1838–1910)
Daughter of Charles Molyneux, 3rd Earl of Sefton, married Hugh Richard Dawnay, 8th Viscount Downe in 1869. Joined the RSN Council some time before March 1877.[322]

Lady Caroline Hamilton-Gordon (née Herschel) (1830–1909)
Eldest daughter of the mathematician and astronomer Sir John Herschel;

married General Sir Alexander Hamilton-Gordon in 1852. Joined the RSN Council some time before April 1873.[323]

Lady Charlotte Schreiber (née Bertie) (1812–1895)
Translator, businesswoman and collector (mainly of china), eldest child of Albemarle, 9th Earl of Lindsey; married first John Guest (d. 1852) in 1833 and second Charles Schreiber in 1855. Actively involved in the RSN from its foundation; Council member until at least July 1875; joined the Managing Committee as an honorary member some time before June 1879.[324]

Charlotte Spencer (née Seymour), Countess Spencer (1835–1903)
Youngest daughter of Lady Augusta and Frederick Seymour; married John Poyntz Spencer, 5th Earl Spencer in 1858. Elected to the RSN Council in January 1875.[325]

Lady Sarah Spencer (1838–1919)
Younger daughter of Frederick Spencer, 4th Earl Spencer. Member of the Managing Committee by April 1878.[326]

Mrs Jane Stuart Wortley (née Lawley) (1820–1900)
Philanthropist, only daughter of Paul Beilby Lawley Thompson, Baron Wenlock; married James Archibald Stuart Wortley, Lady Welby's uncle, in 1846. Joined the Managing Committee as an honorary member some time before June 1879.[327]

Lady Victoria Welby Gregory (née Stuart Wortley) (1837–1912)
Daughter of Charles James Stuart Wortley, married William Welby (later Sir William Welby Gregory, 4th bnt) in 1863. Founder of the RSN. Resigned from the School Council in July 1877; re-elected to the Managing Committee July 1878.[328]

Mrs Madeline Wyndham (née Campbell) (1835–1920)
Daughter of Sir Guy Campbell; married Percy Wyndham, youngest surviving son of George, 1st Baron Leconfield, in 1860. Actively involved in the RSN from its foundation; Council member throughout the 1870s.[329]

Finance Committee Members, 1880
(listed alphabetically by surname)

Michael Biddulph (1834–1923)
Partner in the banking firm Cocks, Biddulph & Co, Liberal MP for Herefordshire 1865–1885. Received a barony in 1903. Member of the Finance Committee by April 1878.[330]

Adelbert Brownlow-Cust, 3rd Earl Brownlow (1844–1921)
Second son of John Hume Egerton, Viscount Alford and Lady Marian Alford; married Adelaide Chetwynd-Talbot (see above) in 1868. Succeeded to the earldom of Brownlow in 1867 on the death of his brother. Held various political offices and was Lord Lieutenant of Lincolnshire from 1867 until his death. Trustee of the RSN from May 1874; Council member from before March 1877.[331]

Sir William Henry Gregory (1816–1892)
Politician and colonial governor. Involved in the arrangement and development of the South Kensington collections; trustee of the National Gallery from 1867. Elected to the Finance Committee in February 1879.[332]

Hugh Lupus Grosvenor, Duke of Westminster (1825–1899)
Philanthropist. Contributed £300 towards a guarantee fund in 1874–1875; by 1877 the RSN had borrowed £800 from the Duke. Sat on the RSN Council and was elected to the Finance Committee in 1877. Grosvenor House became the venue for the School's annual summer sales in 1878 and 1882. Appointed Vice-President of the RSN in 1884 on the recommendation of Princess Helena.[333]

Charles Hanbury-Tracy, 4th Baron Sudeley (1840-1922)
Liberal politician, held various political offices. Member of the Finance Committee by April 1878.[334]

Sir Coutts Lindsay (1824-1913)
Artist and watercolourist; founder of the Grosvenor Gallery. Member of the Finance Committee by April 1878.[335]

Edmund Oldfield (1817-1902)

Barrister-at-law (not practising), friend of John Ruskin and founder of the Arundel Society; librarian and honorary fellow of Worcester College, Oxford; fellow of the Society of Antiquaries (1856); assistant keeper of antiquities at the British Museum. Member of the Finance Committee from at least January 1877.[336]

NOTES

1   Originally known as the School of Art Needlework, the RSN received its royal prefix in March 1875 when Queen Victoria consented to become its first patron. Some time before March 1877 Edward, Prince of Wales and his wife, Princess Alexandra of Denmark, joined the Queen as patrons of the RSN (Royal School of Needlework, Hampton Court Palace, Surrey, RSN Archive 136/18 Catalogue of the Special Exhibition of Needlework executed at the Royal School of Art Needlework [1877]). The word 'Art' was dropped from the title in 1922.

2   Susan Petrilli, 'Welby, Victoria Alexandrina Maria Louisa, Lady Welby (1837–1912)', *Oxford Dictionary of National Biography* (*Oxford DNB*) (Oxford University Press, 2004) [www.oxforddnb.com/view/article/38619, accessed 10 May 2009]. She married the Lincolnshire MP, William Earle Welby, in 1868 and became Lady Welby seven years later when her husband succeeded to the baronetcy.

3   RSN Archive 136/5 Brochure for the School of Art Needlework [October 1873].

4   Mary Schoeser, *English Church Embroidery 1833–1953*, 2nd edn (Watts & Co Ltd, London, 1998), pp 94–95.

5   RSN Archive 164 Brochure for the School of Art Needlework [1874], italic author's.

6   On the role of the aristocracy in organised philanthropy, see K D Reynolds, *Aristocratic Women and Political Society in Victorian Britain* (Clarendon Press, Oxford, 1998), pp 110–19.

7   Initially the staff were expected to work eight hours per day but this was reduced as the 'continued strain of mind and eye was too great on the workers' (*Vice President's Report to H R H The President and The Council of The Royal School of Art Needlework for 1875* (London, 1876), p. 5). Having found that the original entrance fee of £3 was insufficient to cover the cost of training and materials, the figure was soon raised to £5.

8   *The Museums Area of South Kensington and Westminster, Survey of London*, XXXVIII (The Athlone Press, University of London, London, 1975), p. 231. The RSN had very quickly outgrown the premises at 38 Sloane Street and in May 1873 moved into a house a few doors away at no. 31, but within a few months this likewise proved too cramped to accommodate the ever-increasing number of workers.

9   *Vice President's Report*, pp 2–3.

10 Aymer Vallance, 'The Royal School of Art Needlework', *The Magazine of Art*, 20 (1896–97), pp 243–48, at p. 248.

11 Miss Gemmell to Lady Welby, 30 July 1877, private collection. Born in Lanarkshire in 1839, Elizabeth Gemmell was the daughter of a Scottish merchant and one of the first members of the RSN (The National Archives (TNA), Census Returns for England and Wales 1881, RG11/0104 fol. 74 p. 6; RSN Archive 17 Admission Register (1872–1922), p. 131).

12 Virginia Surtees, 'Egerton, Marianne Margaret, Viscountess Alford [*known as* Lady Marian Alford] (1817–1888)', *Oxford DNB* [www.oxforddnb.com/view/article/342, accessed 20 March 2009]. Lady Alford noted in her diary on 19 August that she had received a letter from Miss Gemmell informing her that 'she will [not] write the manual but that she is going to do something else' (Lincolnshire Archives (LA), Brownlow personal papers, Diary of Lady Marian Alford (1877)). Miss Gemmell's refusal was due in part to the fact that she and two of her colleagues were in the process of forming The Decorative Needlework Society, run on similar lines to the RSN, which opened in the autumn of 1877. Miss Gemmell was later described in 1901 as 'Managing dir. Needlework Soc.' (TNA, Census Returns for England and Wales 1901, RG13/87 fol. 66 p. 18).

13 Lady Welby to Lady Alford, no date, private collection.

14 Born at Clareborough in Nottinghamshire in *c*1835, Mary Elliott Brooks married Arthur Scrivenor, vicar of the Lincolnshire parishes of Alvingham (united with Cockerington) and later Horncastle, on 31 December 1857 (www.gilliat1.50megs.com/catalog.html, Descendants of John Gilliat, Generation no. 2/4/19; TNA, Census Returns for England and Wales 1871, RG10/3407 fol. 15 p.1; Census Returns for England and Wales 1881, RG11/3248 fol. 50 p. 23). The Society was run on similar lines to the RSN, though all of its members worked from home; see *The Queen*, 59, p. 173 (11 March 1876); *The Queen*, 62, p. 31 (14 July 1877); *The Queen*, 72, p. 4 (19 July 1881).

15 *The Queen*, 59, p. 173 (11 March 1876). See, for example, the review of the exhibition and sale at the Institute of Art, 9 Conduit Street, London, on 6 March 1880 (*The Queen*, 67, p. 217). Mrs Scrivenor's regular contributions to the newspaper were published under the name 'Mrs Elliott'. The Society for the Employment of Ladies of Small Means was disbanded in 1882, following the death of the Rev. Scrivenor, but according to Dorinda's *Needlework for Ladies, for Pleasure and Profit* (London, 1883), 'Mrs Elliott's Work Society…will be modelled on an entirely new system, as soon as circumstances permit. Mrs Elliott now resides near London, and it is her intention to work the Society on strictly business principles, and on the same plan as the very successful Society in New York [the Society of Decorative Art founded by Candace Wheeler in 1877], as soon as a suitable position and manager can be found. She still employs a certain number of ladies, and allows others to send work to her for sale' (p. 118). For more information on the New York Society, see Candace Wheeler, *The Development of Embroidery in America* (Harper and Bros, New York and London, 1921), chpt. 6.

16 Mary Elliott Scrivenor to Lady Welby, 5 November 1877, private collection.

17 Lady Alford to Lady Welby, Thursday 15th [November 1877], private collection.

18 Lady Welby to Lady Alford, nd, private collection. Lady Welby was also convinced that Mrs Scrivenor could call upon the assistance of Captain George Wündt 'whose extensive knowledge of the subject (both the history as well as the practical parts of it) is well known' (*ibid*). The son of a lieutenant-general in the Würtemberg army, Wündt (1828–1895) had enjoyed a distinguished military career. Following his retirement as Governor of the Ludwigsburg Military School, he settled in London where he joined the art department of *The Queen* in 1873 (*The Sketch*, X/119, p. 68 (8 May 1895); TNA, Census Returns for England and Wales 1881, RG11/187 fol. 85 p. 24).

19 Mrs Scrivenor published several handicraft books including *The Book of Jerseys* (*The Queen*, 71, p. 141 (5 February 1881)), *Collections of Knitting and Crochet Receipts* (Edinburgh, 1896, 2nd edn 1899, 3rd edn 1903, 4th edn 1908), *Weaving at Home, and Indian Knotting* (London, [1908]) and *The New Method of Weaving Scarves, Bags, Book Covers, and other Articles* (Nottingham, [1909]), in addition to numerous supplements printed in *The Queen* (see, for example, her piece on straw work, *The Queen*, 59, p. 361 (27 May 1876) and the set of embroidery designs for antimacassars or chair covers, *The Queen*, 64, p. 111 (17 August 1878)).

20 RSN Archive 130 Case as Sent to Counsel for Opinion (1882), p. 1; see p. 24 below.

21 www.rootsweb.ancestry.com/cgi-bin/igm.cgi?op=AHN&db=:907399&id=I0353, Shelley Lock family trees, Generation no. 1, Thomas Housman Higgin (1788–1861).

22 'Townships: Lancaster', *A History of the County of Lancaster*, 8 (1914), pp 33–48, www.british-history.ac.uk/report.aspx?compid=53258, date accessed: 01 March 2009; www.britarch.ac.uk/lahs/tour/White%20Cross.htm, White Cross Mills; E R Yerburgh, *Some Notes on our Family History* (Constable & Co Ltd, London, 1912), p. 191. Housman later became manager of the County Down Railway in Ireland.

23 See note 21. RSN Archive 17, p. 118. There is some discrepancy over Sarah Anne's date of birth. Yerburgh, for example, cites 1826 (*Some Notes*, p. 195).

24 See note 21. RSN Archive 17, p. 118.

25 RSN Archive 17, p. 118. Two of Letitia's nieces, Ethel and Agnes Higgin, also joined the RSN in April 1881 (RSN Archive 17, p. 166).

26 RSN Archive 116 Finance Committee Minutes (1878–1885), 15 February 1879, fol. 7.

27 RSN Archive 130 Case as Sent to Counsel, p. 1.

28 RSN Archive 117 Managing Committee Minutes (1877–1882), 25 March 1879, fol. 20. John Van der Kiste, 'Helena, Princess [Princess Christian of Schleswig-Holstein] (1846–1923)', *Oxford DNB* [www.oxforddnb.com/view/article/41067, accessed 30 March 2009]. Princess Helena was President of the RSN from the winter of 1872/3 until her death.

29 RSN Archive 130 Case as Sent to Counsel, p. 1.

30 Renamed the Victoria and Albert Museum in 1899.

31 Ruari McLean, *Joseph Cundall: a Victorian Publisher* (T A Constable Ltd, Edinburgh, 1976), p. 44.

32 Low's partner, Edward Marston, later recalled that '[Cundall] assisted us in bringing out many of the finely illustrated works for which our house has been well known' (Edward Marston, *After Work: Fragments from the Workshop of an Old Publisher* (William Heinemann and Charles Scribner's Sons,

London and New York, 1904), p. 104). See, for example, *Hans Holbein* (1879; rep. 1892); *Illustrated Biographies of the Great Artists*, 39 vols (1879–1891); *Annals of the Life & Work of Shakespeare* (1886); and *A Brief History of Wood Engraving from its Invention* (1895).

33 'Some London Publishers. VI. Messrs Sampson Low, Marston, and Co', *The Sketch*, IX/107, pp 135–36 (13 February 1895); G. C. Boase, 'Low, Sampson (1797–1886)', rev. M. Clare Loughlin-Chow, *Oxford DNB* [www.oxforddnb.com/view/article/17075, accessed 2 March 2009]; Rosemary Mitchell, 'Palliser, Fanny Bury (1805–1878)', *Oxford DNB* [www.oxforddnb.com/view/article/21164, accessed 2 March 2009]. Lady Alford returned to Sampson Low & Co in 1886 for the publication of her magnum opus, *Needlework as Art*, see below, p. 34.

34 See, for example, the copy held at Princeton University Library, call number NK8804.H53. I am grateful to Charles E Greene, Librarian in the Manuscripts, Rare Books & Special Collections Department, for checking the imprint.

35 See Charles Scribner's Sons: An Illustrated Chronology (http://library.princeton.edu/libraries/firestone/rbsc/aids/scribner/) for a history of the firm.

36 The firm of Bartlett and Welford is discussed in Donald C Dickinson, *Dictionary of American Antique Bookdealers* (Westport, Connecticut & London, 1998), pp 9–10. Marston, *After Work*, pp 81–83.

37 RSN Archive 130 Case as Sent to Counsel, pp 1–2.

38 TNA, Copy 1/652 Copyright Office Entry Forms (July–September 1882), entry dated 1st August.

39 During the 1870s, around 60% of books retailed at 3s 6d or under ('British Publishing 1800–1900', *Aspects of the Victorian Book*, 'Book Prices 1811–1895', www.bl.uk/collections/early/victorian/pu_intro.html). See, for example, the entries in the *Pall Mall Gazette* and *The Times*, 28 January 1880 and *The Graphic*, 31 January 1880.

40 Higgin, *Handbook of Embroidery*, p. [108].

41 'Chiswick: Economic history', *A History of the County of Middlesex*, 7, *Acton, Chiswick, Ealing and Brentford, West Twyford, Willesden* (1982), pp 78–86, www.british-history.ac.uk/report.aspx?compid=22563, date accessed: 17 March 2009; Janet Ing Freeman, 'Whittingham, Charles (1795–1876)', *Oxford DNB* [www.oxforddnb.com/view/article/29327, accessed 17 March 2009].

42 Ronald B McKerrow, *An Introduction to Bibliography for Literary Students* (Oak Knoll Press, New Castle, Delaware, 1994), pp 300–304.

43 *The Graphic*, 17 April 1880.

44 Anne Anderson, 'A Golden Girl: Burne-Jones and Mary Stuart Wortley', *The Journal of William Morris Studies*, 13/1 (Autumn 1998), pp 64–71, at p. 67. She later described herself as 'a youthful helper to my cousin Lady Welby in the early years of the School' (Mary Countess Lovelace to Lady Smith Dorrien, 10 June 1932, private collection). Her artistic career came to an end when her husband, Ralph Lord Wentworth, succeeded to the Lovelace estates in 1893, though she continued to promote artists and designers.

45 Walter Crane, *An Artist's Reminiscences* (Methuen & Co, London, 1907), p. 164; Caroline Dakers, *Clouds The Biography of a Country House* (Yale University Press, New Haven and London, 1993) and *The Holland Park Circle: Artists and Victorian Society* (Yale University Press, New Haven and London, 1999).

46 RSN Archive 210 Art Committee Minutes (1875–1883), 25 March 1879, fol. 7a, item no. 7.

47 No information has come to light regarding the source of the RSN motto; see the bookplate in Lady Alford's copy of Charles H Hartshorne, *English Mediæval Embroidery* (London, 1848) which contains a variant on the wording, 'A *small* bird may fly high', (RSN Archive/books/En1). The Art Committee resolved at its meeting on 28 March 1879 to use 'the ordinary School monogram' for the *Handbook* (RSN Archive 210, fol. 8). Lady Alford wrote in an undated letter addressed to Lady Welby, 'I have also done a monogram which is not nearly so pretty as Col. Wortley's [Lady Welby's brother, Col Archibald Stuart Wortley]', adding a rough draft of her design (Lady Alford to Lady Welby, private collection). For information on Col. Wortley, see Katherine DiGiulio, *Natural Variations: Photographs by Colonel Stuart Wortley*, exhibition catalogue (Huntington Library, San Marino, California, 1994).

48 Jeremy Paxman, *The Victorians: Britain Through the Paintings of the Age* (BBC Books, London, 2009), pp 108–109.

49 Mrs Bury Palliser, 'The School of Art Needlework', *The Art Journal*, 29 (1877), p. 213.

50 See Patricia Zakreski, *Representing Female Artistic Labour 1848–1890: Refining Work for the Middle-Class Woman* (Ashgate, Aldershot, 2006), chapter 1 'Needlework and Creativity in Representations of the Seamstress'.

51 J Stewart, 'Art Decoration: A Suitable Employment for Women', *The Art Journal*, 12 (1860), pp 70–71, at p. 70.

52 Found on a recent handwritten valuation tucked into one of the RSN copies of the *Handbook*.

53 Higgin, *Handbook of Embroidery*, p. [v].

54 *The Queen*, 67, p. 121 (7 February 1880); RSN Archive 130 Case as Sent to Counsel, p. 1. Lady Alford was later convinced that Miss Higgin's contribution to the drawings was considerably less than she purported.

55 RSN Archive 130 Case as Sent to Counsel, p. 1.

56 TNA, Census Returns for England and Wales 1881, RG11/662 fol. 96 p. 8; J M Rigg, 'Pollock, Sir (Jonathan) Frederick, first baronet (1783–1870)', rev. Partrick Polden, *Oxford DNB* [www/oxforddnb.com/view/article/22479, accessed 27 Oct 2008].

57 RSN Archive 17, p. 93. In 1880, Mary married William Poole, a natural science teacher from Wells, Northants. Following her departure from the RSN in 1883, she continued to design occasionally for the institution. By the turn of the century she was running a private boarding school in Godalming, Surrey (TNA, Census Returns for England and Wales 1901, RG13/606 fol. 86 p. 22).

58 *The Times*, 11 September 1880. Martin Davies, *Aldus Manutius Printer and Publisher of Renaissance Venice* (The British Library, London, 1995), pp 15, 23. Ornamental headpieces based on the work of sixteenth-century English and continental printers are found in a number of books produced by the Chiswick Press.

59 RSN Archive 117, fol. 27.

60 RSN Archive 116, 15 July 1879, fol. 17.

61 RSN Archive 210, 25 March 1879, fol. 7a, item no. 7.

62 *The Queen*, 67, p. 121 (7 February 1880); RSN 130 Case as Sent to Counsel, p. 1.

63 Philip Gaskell, *A New Introduction to Bibliography* (Oak Knoll Press, New Castle, Delaware, rep. 2007), p. 270. Contrary to the glowing review printed in *The Queen*, many of the colour images are out of register; see, for example, plate 21 where none of the colours matches up with the original line image. Furthermore, some of the black and white plates are faulty; for example, in Plate 4 the pattern overruns the background and the centre join is clearly visible. I am grateful to Paul Petzold for his advice on the plates.

64 See, for example, the edition of *Shakespeare's Songs and Sonnets*, designed by Cundall in 1862 (McLean, *Joseph Cundall*, p. 38).

65 For the history of the firm, see Kathy Kajander Tidman, *Art for the Victorian Household* (Online Originals, London & Bordeaux, 1997), part I, 'A Lithographic House: Day & Son Ltd', pp 13–77.

66 *The Queen*, 67, p.121 (7 February 1880). *Myra's Journal of Dress and Fashion* echoed the sentiments expressed in *The Queen*, describing the School as 'the fountain head of Art Needlework': 'A better guide could scarcely be had; every sentence conveys some pithy and practical hint, the meaning of which is made still clearer by illustrations' (1st March 1880, p. 146). Positive reviews also appeared in the American press. The *New York Times*, for example, commented, 'It is a pretty and useful little manual, embellished with plates of original designs in colors' (14 March 1880, p. 8).

67 Higgin, *Handbook of Embroidery*, pp [v], vii–viii.

68 *The Queen*, 61, p. 272 (21 April 1877).

69 The volume contains only brief instructions for working 'embroidery or long stitch' (a combination of stem and long and short stitch), French knot, satin, chain and herringbone stitch in the belief that 'the simpler and the fewer [the stitches], the better the work' (*Art Embroidery*, pp 39–45).

70 *The Queen*, 67, p. 121 (7 February 1880). Within a few weeks after the publication of the *Handbook*, Elizabeth Glaister published in MacMillan & Co's 'Art at Home' series her second volume on art embroidery entitled *Needlework* (London, 1880). The volume was listed in 'The Times Column of New Books and New Editions' on 23 March 1880. Its purpose was to assist women in producing their own designs, 'to give suggestions for the choice of pattern and colour, and to point out some of the ways in which decorative needlework should be applied' (p. 7).

71 *The Queen*, 67, p. 121 (7 February 1880).

72 Higgin, *Handbook of Embroidery*, pp vi, [107]. On the subject of prepared work, see p. 28 below. The RSN's earliest recorded design released to the public – a bellows cover – was printed in the American women's weekly fashion newspaper, *Harper's Bazar*, on 15 January 1881 (XIV/3, p. 36).

73 Mrs Dolby, who was married to the artist Edwin Thomas Dolby (*c*1824–1902), was listed in the 1861 Census as 'Artist Painter in Water Colors (*sic*)' (London Metropolitan Archives, St Pancras Parish Church, Register of Marriages, P90/PANL, Item 097; TNA, Census Returns for England and Wales 1861, RG9/119 fol. 100 p. 8). She later described herself as vestment maker and 'late embroideress to the Queen' (Anastasia Dolby, *Church Embroidery Ancient and Modern* (Chapman and Hall, London, 1867), title-page and *Church Vestments: Their Origin, Use, and Ornament* (Chapman and Hall, London, 1868), p. iii).

74 Lady Welby wrote to Mrs Dolby on 18 January 1873, 'Please let the first lesson…be tracing[,] pricking[,] pouncing & marking', private collection. The prick and pounce method is described in detail in Dolby, *Church Embroidery*, pp 103–104. Lady Welby later sought the advice of the church furnishers and decorators Tattersall & Co on the best means of transferring patterns, and received the following reply: 'We should think that a stencil plate would best answer the purpose such a plate as is used for printing directions, labels etc. Mess[rs] Brown of Manchester use wood blocks for stamping their Communion Linen but these are often not very accurate. The French people have a method of using for pounce some mixture of resin and color (*sic*). This mixture is rubbed over the pricked pattern and then a hot iron placed over it. This fixes the pattern. We have tried it but never found it answer' (Edward Tattersall to Lady Welby, 10 October 1873, private collection). For alternative transfer methods, see Lockwood and Glaister, *Art Embroidery*, pp 50–52 and Glaister, *Needlework*, pp 27–29. The RSN continued to use the prick and pounce method for marking the ground in appliqué; see Higgin, *Handbook of Embroidery*, p. 56 where the technique is described.

75 See also the sections 'Materials to work upon' and 'Materials for working with' in Elvina M Courbould's booklet, *Embroidery and Art Needlework Designs* (Hatchards, London, 1879), pp 3–4. For more information on the author, see George C B Poulter, *The Courbould Genealogy* (Suffolk Institute of Archaeology, Ipswich, 1935), p. 25.

76 *The Queen*, 67, p. 146 (14 February 1880), 'Decorative Needlework' by L[etitia] H[iggin].

77 *The Queen*, 67, p. 146. Miss Higgin's comments were repeated in *Woman's Handiwork in Modern Homes* by the American author Constance C Harrison (Charles Scribner's Sons, New York, 1881), pp 3–4.

78 *Reports of the Hon. Manager and Treasurer to the Council* (1874) p. 6, private collection. For example, over a twelve-month period beginning in April 1876 the RSN spent in excess of £425 with Appleton Bros (RSN Archive 109 Receipts and Payments (1876–77)).

79 *The Queen*, 67, p. 146. In the 1870s aniline dyes, the first synthetic dyes produced on the commercial scale, were still in their infancy, although the first generation of industrial chemists in Britain and Germany were rapidly developing new colours. These new synthetic dyes gave bright shades not previously available, especially on wool and silk. Dyeing on cotton remained difficult and unreliable until towards the end of the century. Many of the new colours had variable resistance to light and washing in comparison to madder and indigo. At worst, the new dyes could even poison the wearer or laundress through the presence of chemicals such as arsenic residue, left in the material, which became active when wet through rain damage, perspiration or washing (Simon Garfield, *Mauve, How One Man Invented a Colour that Changed the World* (Faber & Faber, London, 2000); K G Ponting, *A Dictionary of Dyes and Dyeing* (Bell & Hyman, London, 1981), pp 161–70; Anthony S Travis, *The Colour Chemists* (London, Brent Schools and Industry Project, London, 1983)). I am grateful to Susan Kay-Williams for this information.

80 *The Queen*, 67, p. 146; Higgin, *Handbook of Embroidery*, pp 3–4.

81 *Reports of the Hon. Manager and Treasurer to the Council*, p. 6; RSN Archive 109. Mrs Dolby regarded the old established firm of Pearsall & Co to be the best manufacturer of silk threads (*Church Embroidery*, p. 157).

82 *The Queen*, 67, p. 146.

83 Higgin, *Handbook of Embroidery*, pp 5–7; *The Queen*, 67, p. 146. According to the *Handbook*, thread manufacturers intended doing away with the distinction between rope and fine silk in favour of one uniform thickness of eight strands (p. 6). The RSN sold embroidery silks, filoselle and crewels in

a wide range of colours in small skeins up to ¼-pound bundles at a rate of between 2d and 8s each depending on the thread (RSN Archive 136/35 Prospectus for the Glasgow branch of the RSN [1880], p. 11). No mention is made in the *Handbook* of Chinese floss and embroidery silks, though both were available from the School by 1880 (*ibid*).

84 Higgin, *Handbook of Embroidery*, pp [8]–9; Dolby, *Church Embroidery*, chpt. 10; Lambert, *Handbook*, chpt. 6.

85 The events that led to the signing of the treaty in 1858 and its impact on Japan's export trade are discussed in Sir Hugh Cortazzi, *Britain and the 'Re-opening' of Japan: The Treaty of Yedo in 1858 and the Elgin Mission* (Japan Society Publications, London, 2008). According to Schoeser, Japanese gold thread was introduced into England sometime between 1870 and 1875 (*English Church Embroidery*, pp 15, 106). The 1880 RSN Christmas sale included photograph albums embroidered in 'silk and Japanese gold thread with conventional designs in ancient and modern style' (*The Queen*, 68, p. 575 (18 December 1880)).

86 See for example, Dolby, *Church Embroidery*, pp 136–37. The *Handbook* includes two recipes for preserving gold 'for a certain time' and recommends Mrs Dolby's method of placing cloves in the papers in which gold thread is kept (pp 9–[10]).

87 Lady Welby, 'Draft proposals for the Council to consider', 21 May 1873, no. 14, private collection; Shipping Receipt from the Peninsular and Oriental Steam Navigation Company, 9 June 1874, private collection; Edward Tattersall to Lady Welby, 16 April 1874, private collection.

88 RSN Archive 136/69 Advertising Brochure [1884]. By the early 1880s Japanese gold thread was available through a number of outlets, including Liberty & Co and Holme & Co (Elizabeth Kramer, 'Japanese inspiration and the 'art' of Victorian art embroidery', *Text*, 37 (2009–10), pp 19–27, at p. 22).

89 Higgin, *Handbook of Embroidery*, p. 4; Dorinda, *Needlework for Ladies*, p.19; *The Queen*, 65, p. 360 (19 April 1879).

90 Higgin, *Handbook of Embroidery*, p. 7. See also Brenda King, *Silk and Empire* (Manchester University Press, Manchester, 2005), pp 154–56 and *Dye, Print, Stitch: Textiles by Thomas and Elizabeth Wardle* (Published by the Author, Macclesfield, 2009), chpt. 3; Anne G Jacques, *Leek Embroidery* (Staffordshire Libraries, Arts and Archives, Stafford, 1990).

91 RSN Archive 136/35, p. 11.

92 Higgin, *Handbook of Embroidery*, p. 19.

93 *Reports of the Hon. Manager and Treasurer to the Council*, p. 6; RSN Archive 109; Mabel Cox, 'Arts and Crafts Workers II. Aldam Heaton', *The Artist* (March 1897), pp 121–27, at p. 122; E H Walpole, *Walpole Bros Ltd A Short History of the Firm* (Dublin, [1920]); Alison Adburgham, *Shops and Shopping 1800–1914*, 2nd edn (Barrie & Jenkins, London, 1981), pp 104–105.

94 Higgin, *Handbook of Embroidery*, p. 15. She later wrote, 'Embroidery of this Tussah on a fabric woven of the same species of silk is especially rich and charming, and would certainly wear as long as the fabric itself, which as all know who have worn Tussah silk dresses, is a very long time' (*The Queen*, 67, p. 146).

95 King, *Dye, Print, Stitch*, pp 19–23.

96 Higgin, *Handbook of Embroidery*, p. 15.

97 Higgin, *Handbook of Embroidery*, pp 12–13; *The Queen*, 67, p. 146. Named after the town where it was first manufactured, Bolton sheeting was used for bedding in English workhouses. Heaton did not share the RSN's enthusiasm for the fabric: 'A few years ago, some of the ladies who commenced the School of Needlework in Kensington, set the fashion of using Bolton sheeting for dresses – and even for embroidered dresses. No doubt there is a proper use for Bolton sheeting, though it may not yet have been found – unless it be to make sheets for paupers; but a viler misuse of a fabric than to make it carry embroidery for dresses was surely never conceived' (John Aldam Heaton, *Beauty and Art* (William Heinemann, London, 1897), p. 130).

98 *The Queen*, 67, p. 146; Higgin, *Handbook of Embroidery*, p. 12.

99 S F A Caulfeild and Blanche C Saward, *The Dictionary of Needlework*, 2 vols, 2nd edn (A W Cowan, London, 1887), II, pp 444–45.

100 Higgin, *Handbook of Embroidery*, pp 51–52. The technique was first introduced into Europe from India *c*1759 (Charles Germain de Saint-Aubin, *Art of the Embroiderer* (1770), trans. Nikki Scheuer (Los Angeles County Museum of Art and David R Godine, Inc., Boston, Mass, 1983), p. 54). However, by the time the *Handbook* was published tambouring was confined mainly to the manufacture of Irish or Limerick lace (Heather Toomer, *Antique Lace* (Schiffer Publishing Ltd, Atglen, PA, 2001), p. 112).

101 Higgin, *Handbook of Embroidery*, p. 32.

102 Glaister, *Needlework*, p. 26.

103 A notable exception is long and short stitch. Today the RSN follows the practice developed in the mid-eighteenth century in which the second and all subsequent rows are worked into the stitches of the previous row, the needle coming up through the thread, in contrast to the technique set out in the *Handbook* where the second row of stitches is worked 'in between the uneven lengths of the edging stitches so as to blend with them', the area then being 'filled up by other stitches... carried between those already worked' (see Higgin, *Handbook of Embroidery*, pp 29–30 and illustration no. 10).

104 'French Plumetis' is listed in the manual, without instruction, under satin stitch (Higgin, *Handbook of Embroidery*, p. 23). For the Victorian method of working 'French Plumetis' see Mrs Isabella Beeton, *Beeton's Book of Needlework* (Ward, Lock and Tyler, London, [1870]), figs 90–92 and Caulfeild and Saward, *The Dictionary of Needlework*, I, p. 193.

105 Michael Clifton, 'Rock, Daniel (1799–1871)', *Oxford DNB* [www.oxforddnb.com/view/article/23923, accessed 6 May 2009].

106 Higgin, *Handbook of Embroidery*, pp 29, 45. Curiously, the Latin term for appliqué or cutwork, *Opus Consutum*, does not appear in the manual. The medieval stitches are described in Daniel Rock, *Textile Fabrics; A Descriptive Catalogue Of the Collection of Church-vestments, Dresses, Silk Stuffs, Needlework and Tapestries, forming that Section of the [South Kensington] Museum* (Chapman and Hall, London, 1870), pp xcv–xcvi. Rock's terminology also appears in Alan Cole's introduction to the *Catalogue of the Special Loan Exhibition of Decorative Art Needlework made before 1800* (Chiswick Press, London, 1874), p. xi. Several ladies from the RSN sat on the committee to promote this exhibition, staged at the South Kensington Museum in 1873, and to collect specimens (see pp v–viii). The *Handbook* refers to the nomenclature used by the committee though the date of 1872 given for the exhibition is incorrect (see p. 47).

107 Lady Marian Alford later described the technique as 'the best and most economical method for restoration of old embroideries', *Needlework as Art* (Sampson Low, Marston, Searle, and Rivington, London, 1886), p. 221.

108 Higgin, *Handbook of Embroidery*, p. 57.

109 Higgin, *Handbook of Embroidery*, pp 25–26. Josiane Bertin-Guest, *Chinese Embroidery: Traditional Techniques* (B T Batsford, London, 2003), p. 27. Lady Alford despised raised work or 'embroidery on the stamp', commenting 'I have seen no English specimens that are not beneath criticism; they are only funny' (Lady Alford, *Needlework as Art*, pp 389–90, note 1). The form of raised work described in the *Handbook* in which 'the figures were raised over stuffing, and dressed, as it were, in robes made entirely in point lace, or buttonhole stitches, executed in silk', was produced in England during the middle decades of the seventeenth century and not in the reign of James I (1603–1625), as Lady Alford claims (Xanthe Brooke, *The Lady Lever Art Gallery Catalogue of Embroideries* (Alan Sutton Publishing Ltd, Stroud, 1992), pp 8–9).

110 Alford, *Needlework as Art*, p. 395; Higgin, *Handbook of Embroidery*, p. 45; *The Queen*, 67, p. 146.

111 See note 106; Higgin, *Handbook of Embroidery*, p. 58.

112 Higgin, *Handbook of Embroidery*, p. 42. I am grateful to Edwina Ehrman, Curator of Nineteenth Century Textiles and Fashion, for identifying this object and the toilet cover referred to below. For information on Brangwyn, see David Brangwyn, 'William Curtis Brangwyn Architect and Church Embroidery Designer', *Brangwin Family Newsletter* (December 2003), www.hups.net/~lwuth/brangwin/2003_12_newsletter.html; Alan Windsor, 'Brangwyn, Sir Frank William (1867–1956)', *Oxford DNB* [www.oxforddnb.com/view/article/32046, accessed 6 May 2009].

113 For more information on toilet covers, see the entry 'Toilette' in Clive Edwards, *Encyclopedia of Furnishing Textiles, Floorcoverings and Home Furnishing Practices, 1200–1950* (Lund Humphries, Aldershot and Burlington, Vermont, 2007), pp 218–20.

60

114 Higgin, *Handbook of Embroidery*, pp 52–53. See, for example, Lanto Synge, *Art of Embroidery: History, Style and Technique* (Antique Collectors' Club, Woodbridge, rep. 2006), p. 40.

115 School of Art Needlework Prospectus [October 1872], private collection.

116 Lady Welby's refusal to undertake ecclesiastical work won the heartfelt thanks of Sister Winifred, who ran the famous St Katherine's School of Embroidery, Queen Square, London, founded by the Society of St Margaret, East Grinstead in 1870 (Sister Winifred to Lady Welby, 15 March 1873, private collection; Schoeser, *English Church Embroidery*, p. 115). Higgin, *Handbook of Embroidery*, p. vii.

117 RSN Archive 136/43 Draft advertisement announcing the RSN's desire to execute ecclesiastical work from designs supplied to them by architects or artists for church decoration.

118 Rock, *Textile Fabrics*, pp xcviii–ci, reprinted in Lady Alford, *Needlework as Art*, p. 410. The technique is illustrated in May Morris, 'Opus Anglicanum – the Syon Cope', *Burlington Magazine*, 6 (1904–1905), pp 278–85, at p. 285. The section that follows in the *Handbook* on inlaid appliqué makes no mention of specific examples from the South Kensington Museum, but there can be little doubt that Lady Alford had in mind the three pieces of applied work in crimson velvet and yellow silk/satin listed in Rock's catalogue when she wrote, 'This kind of work may be seen in Italian rooms of the seventeenth century' (Higgin, *Handbook of Embroidery*, p. [54]; Rock, *Textile Fabrics*, p. 17 nos 839–41). Rock no. 841 is illustrated in *Embroidery or The Craft of the Needle* (Truslove, Hanson & Comba Ltd, London and New York, 1899), written by W G Paulson Townsend, design master of the RSN (p. 54 and plate 29).

119 The Exhibition of Ancient Needlework was reviewed in the *Daily News* (9 May 1878). The catalogue does not survive among the papers in the RSN Archive, nor has it been possible to trace the embroideries described in the manual.

120 Higgin, *Handbook of Embroidery*, p. 44; see Appendix II.

121 Higgin, *Handbook of Embroidery*, p. 41; Virginia Surtees, 'Baring, Louisa Caroline, Lady Ashburton (1827–1903)', *Oxford DNB* [www.oxforddnb.com/view/article/50780, accessed 7 May 2009]; see also 'Rutland Gardens and South Place: Kent House and the Kent House Estate Development', *Survey of London*, 45, *Knightsbridge* (2000), pp 134–40, www.british-history.ac.uk/report.aspx?compid=45926, date accessed: 7 May 2009. The curtains are described in Harrison's *Woman's Handiwork* as 'made of tawny plush velvet, changing from gold to amber in varying lights, with a powdered…design of poppies and passion–flowers wrought in gold thread. The border, two feet in width, is of dead gold tapestry, with an *appliqué* of velvets and plushes in all the shades gained by changes of light upon the body of the curtain. This beautiful design, taken from an old Venetian model, is outlined with gold and edged on either side by a scroll reproducing the poppies and passion-flowers in a narrow conventionalized border of gold thread' (pp 65–66).

122 Higgin, *Handbook of Embroidery*, p. 44; RSN Archive 164 Brochure for the School of Art Needlework [1874]; Elizabeth Kramer, 'From specimen to scrap: Japanese textiles in the British Victorian interior, 1875–1900', in *Material Cultures, 1740–1920: The Meanings and Pleasures of Collecting*, eds John Potvin and Alla Myzelev (Ashgate Publishing Ltd, Farnham, 2009), pp 129–47, at pp 132, 139, 141.

123 Higgin, *Handbook of Embroidery*, p. 48; Peter Gordon, 'Spencer, John Poyntz, fifth Earl Spencer (1835–1910)', *Oxford DNB* [www.oxforddnb.com/view/article/36209, accessed 8 May 2009]. Harrison, *Woman's Handiwork*, p. 25. See Appendix II.

124 Higgin, *Handbook of Embroidery*, p. 25.

125 Higgin, *Handbook of Embroidery*, p. 48. According to Harrison, Morris's bed hanging, 'the ground heavily worked in blue silk with cushion stitches, throwing the pattern into relief', was exhibited at Philadelphia (*Woman's Handiwork*, pp 24–25). However, the hanging, which cannot be traced, is not listed in the exhibition catalogue (RSN Archive 136/14 Catalogue of Embroideries [March 1876]).

126 Higgin, *Handbook of Embroidery*, pp 44, 49–50. The counterpane is listed in the Philadelphia catalogue, RSN Archive 136/14, no. 71. Both the American fair and Crane's design are discussed below, see pp 21–22, 40–41. RSN Archive 119 Managing Committee Minutes (1875–1876), 15 July 1875, fol. 2.

127 Higgin, *Handbook of Embroidery*, pp 33–34. The chapter on framing is based on Dolby, *Church Embroidery*, pp 121–29. The *Handbook* recommends using a backing of fine cotton or linen lining where the fabric ground is too weak to take the strain of framing and embroidering, whereas today the RSN uses calico.

128 Higgin, *Handbook of Embroidery*, pp 34–35. Lady Welby noted in the back of her copy of Dolby's *Church Embroidery*, 'The best way to fasten a frame is to two chairs back to back; secure it round the backs by elastic bands' (RSN Archive/books/Do1, end leaf). In Fig. 12 the workers are wearing a large apron with a bib to protect their clothing and a pair of linen sleeves 'to prevent the cuffs from fraying or soiling' their work, as recommended in the manual (Higgin, *Handbook of Embroidery*, p. 35).

129 Examples of this kind of frame do not survive in the RSN Textile Collection.

130 Higgin, *Handbook of Embroidery*, pp 59–60.

131 Caulfeild and Saward, *The Dictionary of Needlework*, I, p. 80.

132 John McG. Davies, 'Pullar, Sir Robert (1828–1912)', *Oxford DNB* [www.oxforddnb.com/view/article/61313, accessed 9 May 2009]

133 See, for instance, Dolby, *Church Embroidery*, pp 115–16; Caulfeild and Saward, *The Dictionary of Needlework*, I, p. 197.

134 Higgin, *Handbook of Embroidery*, p. 59.

135 Dolby, *Church Needlework*, p. 107.

136 Dolby, *Church Needlework*, p. 107. Lady Welby's amendments to Mrs Dolby's recipe included 3½ instead of 3 tablespoons of flour to as much powdered resin as will lie on a halfpenny instead of a shilling (RSN Archive/books/Do1, end leaf). Mrs Dolby's recipe was reproduced in Caulfeild and Saward, *The Dictionary of Needlework*, I, p. 197. The latter also recommended a mixture of gum, sugar candy, alum, flour and water, as well as using size instead of gum or resin (*ibid.*).

137 *The Queen*, 67, p. 121.

138 Review dated 17 April 1880.

139 *The Queen*, 55, p. 335 (25 April 1874).

140 RSN Archive 216 School of Art Needlework Minute Book (1873–1875), 28 April 1874, fol. 19.

141 RSN Archive 216, 23 June 1874, fol. 28.

142 RSN Archive 216, fols 74–75.

143 RSN Archive 216, fol. 82.

144 RSN Archive 210, fols 2–3. The Art Committee under Leighton was short-lived. The last recorded meeting was scheduled for 11 August 1875 (*ibid*, fol. 6), though the committee of artists continued to advise the RSN on matters of design until at least the spring of the following year (*The Queen*, 59, p. 209 (25 March 1876)).

145 RSN Archive 216, 4 May 1875, fol. 78.

146 Higgin, *Handbook of Embroidery*, p. 98; Wheeler, *The Development of Embroidery*, p. 107. Two years later the RSN won a silver medal for embroidery at the *Exposition Universelle* in Paris.

147 *The Queen*, 59, p. 209 (25 March 1876).

148 *The Queen*, 59, p. 217 (1st April 1876). Born in Teignmouth, Devon, in 1849, Christiana Creswell was the daughter of a clergyman (TNA, Census Returns for England and Wales 1861, RG9/1400 fol. 14 p. 21). She joined the paint room of the RSN in 1875 and left two years later having gained a scholarship to the National Art Training School (NATS), South Kensington (RSN Archive 17, fol. 132). She was enrolled at NATS from 1876–1878 and on completion of her scholarship became a decorative designer for rooms and windows (*The Museums Area of South Kensington and Westminster*, pp 79, 107–108, 260–61; 'National Scholars at Central School, South Kensington commencing 1863' in *International Health Exhibition. A Catalogue of Manufacturers, Decorations and Designs* (London, 1881)). She married John Jennings, a journalist, in 1880 and was listed in the 1881 Census as a 'Decorative Artist' (TNA, Census Returns for England and Wales 1881, RG11/71 fol. 93 p. 1). She died in March 1896.

149 Born in London in 1850, Rose Phillips joined the RSN at its inception and was listed in the 1881 Census as a 'Designer for Art Needlework (embroideress)' (TNA, Census Returns for England and Wales 1881, RG11/0041 fol. 25 p. 7). A founding member of the Decorative Needlework Society, she later joined the showroom of Aldam Heaton & Co (TNA, Census Returns for England and Wales 1901, RG15/563 fol. 90 p. 10).

150 Mary Gemmell (b. 1845), designer and sculptress, was the younger sister of the work room mistress. She joined the staff at the Decorative Needlework Society and exhibited regularly at the Arts and Crafts Society's Exhibitions (TNA, Census Returns for England and Wales 1901, RG13/87 fol. 66 p. 18; Linda Parry, *Textiles of the Arts & Crafts Movement* (Thames and Hudson, London, 2005), p. 113). 'Characteristics of the International Fair I', *The Atlantic Monthly*, 38/225 (July 1876), pp 85–91, at p. 90. The object in question was probably the screen in musgrave satin embroidered with myrtle, jasmine and wild rose (RSN Archive 136/14, no. 79).

151 Walter Smith, *Examples of Household Taste: The Industrial Art of the International Exhibition* (R Worthington, New York, [1877]), p. 377.

152 Poynter had retired from the Slade professorship in 1875 to take up the appointment of administering the government art system (Alison Inglis, 'Poynter, Sir Edward John, first baronet (1836–1919)', *Oxford DNB* [www.oxforddnb.com/view/article/35600, accessed 7 April 2009]); George Rawson, 'The Arts and Crafts Movement and British Schools of Art', *The Decorative Arts Society Journal*, 28, 'Arts & Crafts Issue' (2004), pp 29–55, at pp 35–36). Mrs Wyndham reported to the Managing Committee on 29 May 1879 that Poynter had agreed to admit four RSN ladies 'to attend his classes on favourable terms' (RSN Archive 117, fol. 25).

153 For details of the curriculum, see *Prospectus of the National Art Training School* (HMSO, London, [185?–1895?]). Anthea Callen is wrong to assert that workers at the RSN did not receive formal training in design methods until the turn of the century, see *Angel in the Studio: Women in the Arts and Crafts Movement 1870–1914* (Astragal Books, London, 1979), p. 102.

154 Mrs Julia Hawthorne, 'South Kensington Royal School of Art Needlework I', *Harper's Bazar*, XIV/3 (15 January 1881), p. 38; Lady Marian Alford, 'Art Needlework', *The Nineteenth Century*, 49 (March 1881), pp 439–49, at p. 441; RSN Archive 210, 15 May 1879, fol. 10.

155 Duke of Northumberland to Lady Welby, 9 May 1873, private collection; Duchess of Northumberland to Lady Welby, 1st November 1873, private collection.

156 Higgin, *Handbook of Embroidery*, p. [98].

157 See for example, the Art Committee discussed earlier, pp 20–21.

158 Higgin, *Handbook of Embroidery*, pp [97]–98.

159 Higgin, *Handbook of Embroidery*, p. 104.

160 RSN Archive 17, p. 7. Miss Wells, the daughter of a clergyman who had died of softening of the brain under most distressing circumstances, leaving a widow, seven daughters and a son 'unprovided for', entered the RSN on 5 November 1872. She was trained by Lady Welby and was considered a 'quick careful worker of appliqué and of stitches in crewel work'. Frances Turner to Lady Welby, 15 October 1873, private collection.

161 Lady Welby to France Turner, 17 October 1873, private collection.

162 RSN Archive 216, fols 12–13.

163 RSN Archive 216, fol. 18.

164 RSN Archive 216, fols 35, 38.

165 RSN Archive 117, 11 September 1877, fol. 1.

166 RSN Archive 136/17 List of Classes in Ornamental Needlework, September 1877.

167 As noted above (see p. 17), the RSN did not undertake church work, commenting in the preface to the *Handbook*, 'we have not felt ourselves called upon to do more than include it in our course of lessons' (p. vii).

168 RSN Archive 136/22 List of Classes in Ornamental Needlework, September 1878.

169 RSN Archive 136/33 Instructions for Teachers, February 1880.

170 *The Scotsman*, 27 September 1879.

171 RSN Archive 216, 23 February 1875, fol. 69.

172 RSN Archive 216, 23 March 1875, fol. 72.

173 *The Queen*, 61, p. 2 (13 January 1877); Patricia Phillips, 'The Queens Institute, Dublin (1861–1881)', in Norman McMillan (ed.), *Prometheus's Fire* (Tyndall Publications, Kilkenny, 2000), pp 446–63.

174 RSN Archive 119, 16 February 1877, fol. 36; *The Queen*, 61, p. 166 (10 March 1877). The exhibition was reviewed in *The Belfast News-Letter* (7 March 1877). The experiment seems to have been short-lived. The Queen's Institute closed its doors in 1881, unable to overcome severe financial difficulties and the loss of support from Dublin's prominent citizens (Phillips, 'The Queen's Institute', p. 461).

Founded in 1882 by the RSN Council member Katrine, Countess Cowper, Vicereine of Ireland, the Royal Irish School of Art Needlework was established 'on a similar basis' to the RSN but independent of it (Anthony Symondson SJ, 'Art Needlework in Ireland', *Irish Arts Review*, 10 (1994), pp 126–35, at p. 126; *The Times*, 23 January 1884, 'Irish Lace-Making', p. 7).

175 *The Queen*, 68, p. 432 (13 November 1880).

176 RSN Archive 117, 24 April 1879, fol. 22.

177 RSN Archive 117, 27 June 1879, fol. 27 and 1st July 1879, fol. 31.

178 *The Scotsman*, 24 September 1879.

179 *Glasgow Herald*, 10 December 1880.

180 *The Scotsman*, 20 November 1880; RSN Archive 83, fols 71, 73–74.

181 Barbara Morris, *Victorian Embroidery* (Herbert Jenkins Ltd, London, 1962), pp 122–23.

182 RSN Archive 216, fol. 12; *Reports of the Hon. Manager and Treasurer to the Council*, p. 10.

183 See p. 42 below for information on Louisa Wade.

184 RSN Archive 216, 7 November 1874, fol. 45.

185 She was the daughter of Captain Martin Haworth and his wife, Lady Mary, later Countess of Rothes (TNA, Census Returns for England and Wales 1871, RG10/89 fol. 50 pp 1–2; Edward J F Tozer, *The South Devon Hunt* (Published by the Author, Teignmouth, 1916), p. 60). Miss Haworth resigned from her post two years later following the re-organisation of the School. By the time the *Handbook* was published the prepared work department was run by Miss Barber (RSN Archive 17, p. 70).

186 Higgin, *Handbook of Embroidery*, p. [100].

187 RSN Archive 136/23 Finished Work [1878]; RSN Archive 23a Prepared Work [1878]; Higgin, *Handbook of Embroidery*, pp 100–102, 105–106.

188 Higgin, *Handbook of Embroidery*, p. [103].

189 *Reports of the Hon. Manager and Treasurer to the Council*, pp 9–10. Capel invested £1200 of his own money in the School and was responsible for arranging the general part of the business, providing the use of a room, building showcases, supplying ground fabrics, taking orders, printing notices, and so on, in return for which he was entitled to 20% of the profits.

190 RSN Archive 216, fols 12–13.

191 Flyer advertising the RSN's agents, *c*1874–1875, private collection; Morris, *Victorian Embroidery*, p. 124.

192 The notion of setting up provincial agencies was first raised at a Council meeting on 23 March 1875 (RSN Archive 216, fol. 73).

193 Higgin, *Handbook of Embroidery*, p. 106. Pierce and Jenkyns of Boston had applied to the RSN in April 1879 to become its first American agent but their offer was declined. The Managing Committee reconsidered the idea of setting up a Boston agency the following November (RSN Archive 117, fols 22, 24, 49).

194 RSN Archive 136/21 Memorandum of Conditions to be subscribed by persons desirous of becoming agents of the Sale of Needlework of the School, 187[?]; RSN Archive 136/32 Memorandum of Conditions to be subscribed by persons desirous of becoming agents of the Sale of Needlework of the School, (188[?]). In June 1879, the RSN issued an advertisement cautioning the public against sales of spurious or pirated designs claiming to be the work of the School (RSN Archive 117, fol. 29–30). A copy of the notice was printed in the *Handbook* (p. [107]).

195 RSN Archive 117, fol. 74.

196 Miss Higgin's name is omitted from the advertisement printed in the 1880 prospectus for the Glasgow branch of the RSN, which reads: 'NEW HANDBOOK OF EMBROIDERY, *EDITED BY* LADY MARIAN ALFORD. By Authority of the Royal School of Art Needlework' (RSN Archive 136/35, p. [15]).

197 Mrs Bayman had joined the RSN in May 1875 as mistress of the appliqué department, having 'learnt her craft in foreign schools' (RSN Archive 216, 4 May 1875, fol. 79; Lady Alford, 'Art Needlework', p. 441). She retired from the RSN on the grounds of ill health in February 1883 (RSN Archive 83 Managing Committee Minutes (1882–1885), fols 17–18). Miss Higgin claimed that Mrs Bayman had not assisted her with the first edition but this was subsequently disproved by a letter that she had sent, dated 4 June 1879, in which she referred to Mrs Bayman as 'overlooking the MSS' (RSN Archive 130 Case as Sent to Counsel, p. 2).

198 TNA, Copy 1/652. The entry form was witnessed by John Rivington on behalf of Sampson Low & Co.

199 TNA, Copy 1/652, entry dated 14 August 1882, witnessed by her older sister, Martha.

200 RSN Archive 130 Case as Sent to Counsel, pp 2–3. Several documents were sent for reference to Counsel, including the original agreement made with Sampson Low & Co, Miss Higgin's case 'as drawn by herself', a letter from Lady Wentworth (formerly Miss Stuart Wortley) dated 6 August 1882, a letter from Hudson & Co addressed to Miss Higgin dated 31 July 1882, the new contract signed by Lady Alford and a copy of the *Handbook*. The original documents and correspondence were available for consultation at Alford House by members of the Managing Committee. Apart from the *Handbook*, none of the supporting material has survived.

201 Stanway House, Glos., Stanway papers (SH), Diary of Mary Constance Wyndham, Lady Elcho (1882–1884), pp 49, 87, 90.

202 For a detailed description of the judgement, see RSN Archive 130 Case as Sent to Counsel, p. 3 and Montagu Muir Mackenzie's 'Opinion' (1882).

203 RSN Archive 83, fols 7–8.

204 RSN Archive 83, 16 November 1882, fols 9–11.

205 RSN Archive 83, fols 9–11; RSN Archive 130 Assignment of Copyright of The Handbook of Embroidery, 27 January 1883.

206 RSN Archive 83, fol. 26.

207 RSN Archive 83, 19 April 1883, fols 28–29 and 24 May 1883, fols 32–33; RSN Archive 79 Finance Committee Agenda Book (1881–1885), 24 May 1883, fol. 20.

208 RSN Archive 83, fols 33–34.

209 RSN Archive 83, 15 November 1883, fols 45–46; LA, Diary of Lady Marian Alford (1883), entry dated 17 July.

210 Higgin, *Handbook of Embroidery*, p. vii; RSN Archive 83, fol. 48. No evidence of the second edition of the *Handbook* is known to have survived.

211 RSN Archive 83, fols 49–50.

212 RSN Archive 83, fols 50–52.

213 RSN Archive 79 Finance Committee Agenda Book (1881–1885), 10 December 1883, fol. 25–25v.

214 LA, Diary of Lady Marian Alford (1884), entry dated 5 January; RSN Archive 83, 15 January 1884, fols 55–56.

215 LA, Diary of Lady Marian Alford (1884), entry dated 19 March; Lady Alford, *Needlework as Art*, p. vii.

216 Review dated 3 March 1886. See also LA, BNLW 4/8/2/6, Album containing reviews of Lady Marian Alford's *Needlework as Art*, published January 1886.

217 RSN Archive 83, 18 June 1884, fols 68–69. She had been elevated to the post of secretary in March 1882 and awarded a pay rise four months later (RSN Archive 117, 17 March 1882, fol. 71; RSN Archive 83, 20 July 1882, fol. 5).

218 RSN Archive 83, 7 July 1884, fols 71–72.

219 RSN Archive, 18 July 1884, fol. 76.

220 *Woman's Penny Paper*, 5 November 1890.

221 See her articles on English decorative needlework and the Leek Embroidery Society's facsimile of the Bayeux tapestry, *The Art Journal*, new series (April–May 1886), pp 121–26 and 139–44 and *Magazine of Art*, 10 (1887), pp 43, 151, 345–48; *The Scotsman*, 3 November 1885.

222 TNA, Census Returns for England and Wales 1901, RG13/1161 fol. 75 p. 40. *Margaret Grantley. A Study in Black and White* (1885), *A Cornish Maid* (1896), *Cousin Jem, a Sepia Sketch* (1897) and *Lyona Grimwood, Spinster* (1900). *Spanish Life in Town and Country* (1902) is erroneously attributed to Louis Higgin. Miss Higgin died in December 1913, aged 76.

223 Prior to the Berne Convention of 1886 there was no international copyright agreement between the United States and Britain which meant that an American publisher could publish a British book without permission of the author (Tim Padfield, *Copyright for Archivists and Records Managers*, 3rd edn (Facet Publishing, London, 2007), p. 10).

224 By the end of the nineteenth century, five RSN-trained teachers superintended the decorative art societies in New York, Philadelphia, Boston, Chicago and San Francisco (RSN Archive 136/104

Royal School of Art Needlework Prospectus [1892]); Wheeler, *The Development of Embroidery*, p. 117). For example, Frances Lawe took charge of the art needlework school in Philadelphia in 1878 (RSN Archive 17, p. 119; RSN Archive 117, p. 3; Higgin, *Handbook of Embroidery*, p. 99) followed shortly by Mrs Pode, who became head of the Society of Decorative Art in New York (Candace Wheeler, *Yesterdays in a Busy Life* (Harper and Brothers, New York and London, 1918), pp 220–21; RSN Archive 17, p. 45).

225 Morris, *Victorian Embroidery*, pp 183, 188–89; Higgin, *Handbook of Embroidery*, p. 106; RSN Archive 136/46 Advertising card with a list of agents in Britain and North America [1881]; Doreen Bolger Burke *et al*, *In Pursuit of Beauty. Americans and the Aesthetics Movement* (Metropolitan Museum of Art, New York, 1986), p. 418.

226 See, for example, the firm's advertisement in *Harper's Bazar*, XII/15, 12 April 1879, p. 243.

227 Several of the stitch diagrams from the *Handbook* were also reproduced without acknowledgement in Harrison's *Woman's Handiwork* of 1881, see pp 20–22, 24, 29–31, 33, 35, 37–38, 40, 43.

228 Higgin, *Handbook of Embroidery*, p. 29; Lucretia P. Hale (ed.), *Art Needlework for Decorative Embroidery*, 2nd edn (S W Tilton & Co, Boston, 1881), pp 10 (n. 1), 13.

229 I am grateful to Kathy Woodrell, Reference Specialist, Decorative Arts, Library of Congress, Washington DC for her assistance in checking the 1880 Boston edition.

230 Kate Gannett Wells, 'Women in Organization', *The Atlantic Monthly*, 46/275 (September 1880), pp 360–68, at p. 361.

231 Vallance, 'The Royal School of Needlework', pp 243, 246, 248.

232 *Daily News* review, 16 October 1880.

233 Stephen Wildman and John Christian, *Edward Burne-Jones Victorian Artist-Dreamer*, exhibition catalogue (Metropolitan Museum of Art, 1998), pp 9–10 (fig. 8), 97–98; Lady Georgiana Burne-Jones, *Memorials of Edward Burne-Jones*, 2 vols (The Macmillan Co, London & New York, 1904), I, p. 276. Around the same time Burne-Jones designed a series of embroideries based on Sir Thomas Malory's *Morte d'Arthur* for his own home at 62 Great Russell St, opposite the British Museum (Linda Parry, 'Textiles', in Linda Parry (ed.), *William Morris*, Victoria and Albert Museum exhibition catalogue (Philip Wilson Publishers Ltd, London, 1996), pp 224–95, at p. 238).

234 Wildman and Christian, *Edward Burne-Jones*, pp 13–14, 16 (fig. 14), 180–81; Parry, 'Textiles', pp 240–41. The partnership of Morris, Marshall, Faulkner & Co was dissolved and reformed as Morris & Co with Morris as the sole owner on 31 March 1875 (Charles Harvey and Jon Press, 'The Businessman', in Parry, *William Morris*, pp 49–57, see pp 49–51).

235 LA, Diary of Lady Marian Alford (1875), entries dated 26 October and 20 November 1875. The *Musicians* hanging in the Victoria and Albert Museum, which has been dated *c*1875, is generally regarded as the earliest design created by the artist for the RSN (Morris, *Victorian Embroidery*, pp 114, 156 (Plate 47); Parry, 'Textiles', p. 242). However, the design is not the work of Burne-Jones but of his contemporary, Selwyn Image, whose lengthy association with the School began in the late 1870s (*The Ladies Field*, 4 November 1899, pp 380–82; RSN Archive D1/509).

236 Review dated 11 March 1876.

237 *Magazine of Art*, III (1880), 'Art Needlework II', pp 178–81, at p. 179. See for example, *The Times*, 23 March 1876 and *The Queen*, 59, p. 209, 'Art Needlework for the Philadelphia Exhibition' (25 March 1876); *The Queen*, 59, p. 217 (1st April 1876).

238 See, for example, *The Atlantic Monthly*, 38/225 (July 1876), pp 85–91, *Harper's Bazar*, IX/41, pp 649–50 (7 October 1876) and Smith, *Examples of Household Taste*.

239 *The Queen*, 61, p. 179, 'Exhibition of the Royal School of Art Needlework' (17 March 1877). The hanging is not listed in the price catalogue that accompanied the Special Exhibition of Needlework executed at the Royal School of Art Needlework (RSN Archive 136/18), though Burne-Jones's name was listed among the exhibited designers.

240 *Magazine of Art*, III (1880), 'Art Needlework IV', pp 428–31, at p. 430.

241 RSN Archive 136/30 Catalogue of the Glasgow Exhibition, 'Modern Embroidery', item no. 17.

242 Higgin, *Handbook of Embroidery*, p. 62. In her article on the revival of decorative needlework, Letitia Higgin later described *Musica* and the classical figures in Selwyn Image's four-panel screen as notable examples of this style (*The Art Journal* (April 1886), p. 123; see below, pp 45–46).

243 *Magazine of Art*, V (1881–82), pp 219–220, at p. 219. *Musica* is cited among the best examples of outline work in Harrison's *Woman's Handiwork*, p. 73.

244 Morris refers to two extant examples of *Musica*, one at 94 Park Lane, occupied by Albert Pemberton & Sons Ltd, and the other in the Walsall Museum, Staffordshire, neither of which can be traced (*Victorian Embroidery*), p. 140.

245 'Needlework design – Study for Poesis/Poetry', Accession no. 1904P190, *c*1873–1875; *Hidden Burne-Jones: Works on Paper by Edward Burne-Jones from Birmingham Museums and Art Gallery*, exhibition catalogue (Giles, London, 2007), p. 77.

246 Wildman and Christian, *Edward Burne-Jones*, pp 278–79. All the rest of Burne-Jones's works copied by the RSN were taken from tapestry designs produced for Morris & Co (*Pomona* and *Flora*) or from the artist's oil paintings (*Sibylla Delphica*, *The Golden Stairs* and *The Mill*). A small panel based on the tapestry design *Angeli Ministrantes* may also be the work of the RSN.

247 Dakers, *Clouds*, pp 40–41, fig. 22; SH, Diary of Mary Constance Wyndham, Lady Elcho (1880–1882), p. 136.

248 'The Needlework of Lady Carew and Mrs Clifford Cory', *Needlecraft* (Christmas 1906), pp 12, 14, 25.

249 I am grateful to Angela Lassig, Senior Curator, Te Papa Tongarewa, Wellington, New Zealand for this information. See www.collections.tepapa.govt.nz/search.aspx?term=Jane%20Cory, registration nos PC004115 and PC004118 for images of the embroideries.

250 See the review in *The Times*, 12 January 1907; RSN Archive 164 Brochure for the Royal School of Art Needlework [*c*1908], containing 'Examples of some of the orders which have been carried out', p. 5. The RSN also produced a twofold screen depicting *Musica* and *Poesis*, see Diana Wyllie, *The History of English Embroidery* (Diana Wyllie Ltd, London, nd), no. 5 'Victorian and Modern Embroidery', item no. 17, present whereabouts unknown.

251 Isobel Spencer, *Walter Crane* (MacMillan Publishing Co Inc, New York, 1975), pp 101–122.

252 RSN Archive 119, 22 July 1875, fol. 3. For example, the screen was the subject of an article printed in *The Ladies Field* on 28 April 1900. Commenting on his relationship with the RSN, Crane noted in his autobiography that many of his designs 'for screens, panels, and other things, in which I introduced figures, birds (notably peacocks), and animals…are still worked, I believe' (*An Artist's Reminiscences*, p. 164).

253 Review dated 11 March 1876.

254 *Harper's Bazar*, IX/41, p. 650.

255 RSN Archive 136/14, no. 32. The suite of embroideries did not find a buyer at the American fair and was offered for sale the following year at the Special Exhibition of Needlework for a total of £370 (RSN Archive 136/18, no. 32).

256 RSN Archive 136/30, nos 18 and 34.

257 Local Studies Department, Kensington Central Library, Crane Portfolios F(1)/18 and G(6)/39.

258 Museum no. T.774 to D–1972. One of the panels is currently on display in the British Galleries. The inscription is translated in Morris, *Victorian Embroidery*, p. 136. This screen may be identified with the one listed in the 1886 inventory of Alford House: 'a large 5 fold screen gilt frame made at Grantham, embroidery from design by Walter Crane from R.S.A.N.', bequeathed to Lady Alford's son, Lord Brownlow (LA, BNLW 2/2/7/11 'Furniture Ornamental Screens, no. 6').

259 See for example, *The Telegraph*, 22 March 1876, *The Times*, 23 March 1876 and *The Queen*, 59, p. 209 (25 March 1876).

260 *The Times*, 11 September 1880, p. 11.

261 The borders printed in the *Handbook* are taken from a set of six botanical studies in the artist's hand painted for the RSN; the others include iris, orange, jessamine and cowslip (RSN Archive D6/7–12). See also the sample cards, RSN Archive D1/23–24, 28.

262 RSN Archive 136/14, no. 16 'Two Pairs Linen Curtains, Border "Daffodil"' and no. 118 'Mantel Valance and Curtain on green Diagonal, with Border of "Yellow Primrose"'. The former was offered for sale at the Special Exhibition of Needlework in March 1877 for £13 (RSN Archive 136/18, no. 16).

263 He had been commissioned by Leighton, for example, to design the artist's house and studio at 2 Holland Park Road (Daniel Robbins and Reena Suleman, *Leighton House Museum* (The Royal Borough of Kensington and Chelsea, London, 2005), pp 17–27).

264 Dakers, *The Holland Park Circle*, pp 124–26.

265 Victorian and Albert Museum, Royal Institute of British Architects Library (RIBA), Victoria and Albert Museum, SC127/1, dated 1st May 1873. Lady Welby received a note from Aitchison dated 25 February 1874 informing her that he had been asked by Mrs Wyndham to call at the School to see the work now being done on her counterpane (G Aitchison to Lady Welby, private collection).

266 RSN Archive 216, fols 19, 74–75.

267 RSN Archive 210, 28 July 1875, fol. 6.

268 RIBA, SC126/6, dated 1st December 1875.

269 The designs are dated 26 and 7–9 October 1876 respectively (RSN Archive D2 fols 27v, 28r–29r). The latter exists in three contrasting colour ways with the directions in Aitchison's hand 'embroidered on blue satin' and 'To be worked in silk or cotton or white cotton'.

270 The quilt did not sell at the American fair and was included in the Special Exhibition of Needlework the following March for £75 (RSN Archive 136/18, no. 65). Higgin, *Handbook of Embroidery*, p. 62.

271 Higgin, *Handbook of Embroidery*, p. 6; RSN Archive 136/18, T.

272 TNA, Census Returns for England and Wales, 1871, RG10/144 fol. 10 p. 13.

273 Lady Welby to Frances Turner, 18 December 1873, private collection. For example, Lady Welby was keen that he should 'enlarge the Gambier Parry squares [see RSN Archive D2, fol. 39r] & make quite small drawings of some large Renaissance patterns' (Lady Welby to Frances Turner, 3 December 1873, private collection. Dennis Farr, 'Parry, Thomas Gambier (1816–1888)', *Oxford DNB* [www.oxforddnb.com/view/article/21436, accessed 9 April 2009].

274 TNA, Census Returns for England and Wales 1881, RG11/0129 fol. 96A p. 21; RSN Archive 216, fols 12, 47, 64. Louisa Wade served as manageress of the RSN for over forty years, retiring from the post on 31 March 1915 (RSN Archive 17, p. 312).

275 *Reports of the Hon. Manager and Treasurer to the Council*, p. 9.

276 TNA, Census Returns for England and Wales 1871, RG10/144 fol. 10 p. 13; www.singletonsdiary. wordpress.com/2009/03/04/nugent-wade/, 'Nugent Wade', R C Singleton's Diary (1847): Diary of a Victorian educational reformer; 'St. Anne's Church', *Survey of London*, 33–34, *St Anne Soho* (1966), pp 256–77 www.british-history.ac.uk/report.aspx?compid=41107, accessed 07 June 2008; Lady Welby to Frances Turner, 6 January 1874, private collection.

277 Antonia Brodie *et al* (eds), *Directory of British Architects*, II, 'L–Z' (Continuum, London and New York, 2001), pp 881–82.

278 RSN Archive D2, fols 9r-16ar, 18r-19r.

279 *The Queen*, 59, p. 217 (1st April 1876); *Harper's Bazar*, IX/41, p. 649. Smith included in his *Examples of Household Taste* an illustration of Wade's square stool or ottoman embroidered with jasmine (p. 95). RSN Archive 136/14, nos 3, 9–10, 21, 72–73, 96, 113. None of the objects designed by Wade was purchased at Philadelphia. They were offered for sale at the Special Exhibition of Needlework the following year (RSN Archive 136/18).

280 Higgin, *Handbook of Embroidery*, p. 63.

281 Leslie Gilbert Pine, *The New Extinct Peerage 1884–1971: Containing Extinct, Abeyant, Dormant and Suspended Peerages With Genealogies and Arms* (Heraldry Today, London, 1972), p. 47. Victoria and Albert Museum, no. T.183–1975.

282 RSN Archive 119, 15 Jul 1875, fol. 2. The RSN had first approached Morris, Marshall, Faulkner & Co in December 1872 to enquire if the firm would be interested in having embroidery work done off the premises, but received a cool response from the works manager, George Wardle, who was convinced that Morris would not entertain such an arrangement (Henry Capel to Lady Welby, 17 December 1872, private collection).

283 RSN Archive 210, 28 July 1875, fol. 6.

284 *Harper's Bazar*, IX/41, p. 649. The design cannot be traced.

285 Illustrated in Parry, 'Textiles', p. 241; Higgin, *Handbook of Embroidery*, p. 63. The pattern is very similar to the furnishing textile *Marigold*, manufactured by Thomas Wardle for Morris & Co in 1875 (Parry, 'Textiles', pp 256–57). RSN Archive 136/14, no. 121. The sofa back cover was priced at eight guineas in the March 1877 sale catalogue (RSN Archive 136/18, no. 121).

286 RSN Archive 136/14 no. 111. The screen was offered for sale in the Special Exhibition of Needlework for £230 (RSN Archive 136/18, no. 111). Parry, 'Textiles', p. 259; Linda Parry, *William Morris Textiles* (Weidenfeld and Nicholson Ltd, London, 1983), p. 150 (no. 21). The RSN Archive contains an undated sample card with a pencil drawing of the design labelled 'Morris Honeysuckle' (D1/21). Linda Parry, private communication, 25 November 2009.

287 Parry, 'Textiles', p. 242. The catalogue entry includes an illustration of the hanging, which is now in a private collection.

288 The watercolour design is dated 1874 in Oliver Fairclough and Emmeline Leary, *Textiles by William Morris and Morris & Co. 1861–1940* (Thames and Hudson, London, 1981), p. 89, item no. P19A. However, there is no evidence to corroborate this dating. I am grateful to Victoria Osborne, Curator of Prints and Drawings, Birmingham Museums and Art Gallery for checking the records relating to the design.

289 RSN Archive 136/14, no. 31. The entry in the 1876 catalogue is too vague to identify the design. The hanging was priced at £120 in the Special Exhibition of Needlework (RSN Archive 136/18, no. 31).

290 Lady Welby's notes on the early history of the RSN, nd and 21 May 1873, private collection.

291 School of Art Needlework Prospectus [October 1872], private collection; Henry Capel to Lady Welby, 19 and 24 October 1872, private collection.

292 Francis Jekyll, *Gertrude Jekyll A Memoir* (Jonathan Cape Ltd, London, 1934), p. 87. The venue is misidentified in some secondary sources as the London International Exhibition Society in New Bond Street (Sally Festing, *Gertrude Jekyll* (Penguin Books Ltd, London, 1991), p. 71), founded in 1881. See, for example, her embroidery patterns for Frederic Leighton and the Wyndhams (Jekyll, *Gertrude Jekyll*, p. 87; Dakers, *The Holland Park Circle*, p. 126; SH, Diary of Mary Constance Wyndham, Lady Elcho (1879–1880), pp 150–51 (15 November 1879), 242 (22 March 1880).

293 RSN Archive D1/2 and 34.

294 Harrison, *Woman's Handiwork*, pp 190–91. See also Martha Crabill McClaugherty, 'Household Art: Creating the Artistic Home, 1868–1893', *Winterthur Portfolio*, 18/1 (Spring 1983), pp 1–26, at p. 25.

295 Helen Caroline Jones, 'Image, Selwyn (1849–1930)', *Oxford DNB* [www.oxforddnb.com/view/article/34093, accessed 15 April 2009].

296 See note 235 regarding the *Musicians* hanging. RSN Archive 136/30 'Modern Embroidery', no. 7. Three undated sample cards of the screen panels are preserved at RSN Archive D1/3a–c.

297 In its review of the RSN's annual summer sale and exhibition in 1896, *The Manchester Guardian* commented, 'Nothing…in the whole display was finer than a screen of four panels devoted to outline figures of Juno, Proserpine, Venus and Minerva, executed in gold and olive threads on a cream ground, and framed with appropriate severity in plain but precious woods' (26 June 1896).

298 The screen is illustrated in Lanto Synge, *Antique Needlework* (Blandford Press, London, rep. 1989), p. 148 and Synge, *Art of Embroidery*, p. 281.

299 The panels were formerly in the possession of Richard Scott (Morris, *Victorian Embroidery*, p. 137 and pl. 56).

300 See note 242.

301 I am grateful to Meg Andrews for bringing this embroidery to my attention.

302 RSN Archive 17, p. 160. Miss Whichelo became head designer of the RSN and worked on the coronation regalia of Edward VII, George V and George VI before retiring from the School in 1939 (Nicola Beauman, *Morgan: a Biography of E M Forster* (Hodder and Stoughton, London, 1993), pp 242–43; RSN Archive 17, p. 312).

303 See Fig. 14.

304 There is no record of a Miss Jones with the initials 'J H' among the extant papers of the RSN. The panel is illustrated in Parry, *Textiles of the Arts and Crafts Movement*, p. 129 and in Morris, *Victorian Embroidery*, p. 137 and pl. 55, where the embroidery is dated c1916.

305 Illustrated in Max Donnelly, 'Living with antiques. A collection of British art pottery and fin de siècle decorative arts', *The Magazine Antiques* (June 2008), pp 94–103, at p. 101.

306 TNA, Census Returns for England and Wales 1861, RG9/1257 fol. 160 p. 3.

307 RSN Archive 17, p. 144.

308 Kenneth McConkey, 'Clausen, Sir George (1852–1944)', *Oxford DNB* [www.oxforddnb.com/view/article/32435, accessed 4 April 2009]. Agnes Webster is listed in 1881 as 'Artist Painter' (TNA, Census Returns for England and Wales 1881, RG11/1998 fol. 77 p. 5). Very little of her work survives, apart from some illustrations of children in the verse collection *Daisy Days* (Griffith, Farran & Co, London, [1888]) and a watercolour on paper entitled *The Lazy Boy* (1882) exhibited at the Fine Art Society, London in 2006 (see the *Catalogue*, pp 32–33). She died in March 1944 (McConkey, *op. cit.*).

309 Higgin, *Handbook of Embroidery*, p. 63.

310 Very little is known about her background except that she was the granddaughter of a Custom House official (TNA, Census Returns for England and Wales 1851, HO107/1555 fol. 472 p.4). RSN Archive 17, p. 164.

311 RSN Archive 136/30, nos 12 and 14.

312 RSN Archive D5/39.

313 RSN Archive 17, p. 164. Miss Burnside made her living both as an artist and a poet (TNA, Census Returns for England and Wales 1891, RG 12/452 fol. 86 p. 38). In addition to working for the *Girl's Own Paper*, she published several verse collections, see for example, *Buttercup Pictures* (1899), *The Children's Wonderland* (1900), *The Fairy Ring* (1900) and *Circling Surprises* (1901), and wrote lyrics for the well-known contralto and composer Charlotte Sainton-Dolby (1821–1885), including *The Drummer's Song* ([1874]) and *They often ask why I never sing* ([1876]) (Sophie Fuller, 'Sainton-Dolby, Charlotte (1821–1885)', *Grove Music Online* [www.oxfordmusiconline.com/subscriber/article/grove/music/24331?q=Sainton-Dolby&search=quick&source=omo_gmo&pos=1&_start=1#first hit, accessed 4 April 2009]). From about 1875 Miss Burnside lived with the popular novelist Rosa Nouchette Carey (Charlotte Mitchell, 'Carey, Rosa Nouchette (1840–1909)', *Oxford DNB* [www.oxforddnb.com/view/article/32288, accessed 5 April 2009]).

314 Higgin, *Handbook of Embroidery*, p. 64.

315 *Harper's Bazar*, XIV/3, p. 38 (15 January 1881) and XIV/5, pp 75–76 (29 January 1881).

316 *Harper's Bazar*, XIV/5, p. 76.

317 See above p. 16 and note 106.

318 www.thepeerage.com/p10105.htm#i101048; RSN Archive 136/18.

319 www.thepeerage.com/p7938.htm#i79372; School of Art Needlework Prospectus, April 1873, private collection. Between September 1873 and May 1879, Lady Fitzhardinge spent £101 10s 6d on embroideries made at the RSN, including two sets of curtains and a bell pull (Berkeley Castle, Glos, GBB 177, Steward's Accounts 1870–1879, pp 107, 145, 186, 229–30, 272, 274, 314, 316, 357 and 360). I am grateful to Stephen Price for drawing my attention to this source and to the Berkeley Will Trust for permission to cite the document. Lady Welby to Miss Turner, 30 August 1873; Miss Turner to Lady Welby, 9 October and 19 November 1873, 11 March and August 1874, private collection.

320 www.thepeerage.com/p1277.htm#i12769; *Memorandum and Articles of Association*, p. 15.

321 Allen Warren, 'Cowper, Francis Thomas de Grey, seventh Earl Cowper (1834–1905)', *Oxford DNB* [www.oxforddnb.com/view/article/32599, accessed 11 June 2009]; Symondson, 'Art Needlework in Ireland', p. 126; RSN Archive 136/18. The RSN embroidered in the Chinese style a set of furnishings and hangings for the state bedroom at Panshanger, the Cowpers' Hertfordshire seat (Alford, *Needlework as Art*, p. 398).

322 www.thepeerage.com/p2938.htm#i29375; RSN Archive 136/18.

323 www.thepeerage.com/p2472.htm#i24711; School of Art Needlework Prospectus, April 1873, private collection.

324 Revel Guest and Angela V John, *Lady Charlotte: A Biography of the Nineteenth Century* (Weidenfeld and Nicolson, London, 1989); School of Art Needlework circular [October 1872], private collection; RSN Archive 136/26a Royal School of Art Needlework Prospectus (June 1879).

325 www.thepeerage.com/p10238.htm#i102374; RSN Archive 216, fol. 61.

326 www.thepeerage.com/p10515.htm#i105147; *Memorandum and Articles of Association*, p. 15.

327 Lori Williamson, 'Wortley, Jane Stuart- (1820–1900)', *Oxford DNB* [www.oxforddnb.com/view/article/55213, accessed 15 June 2009]; RSN Archive 136/26.

328 See note 2; RSN Archive 117, fol. 12.

329 School of Art Needlework Prospectus [October 1872], private collection; see also Dakers, *Clouds*.

330 www.thepeerage.com/p1406.htm#i14054; *Memorandum and Articles of Association*, p. 16.

331 www.thepeerage.com/p1277.htm#i12770; RSN Archive 216, fol. 21; RSN Archive 136/18.

332 C. L. Falkiner, 'Gregory, Sir William Henry (1816–1892)', rev. Peter Gray, *Oxford DNB* [www.oxforddnb.com/view/article/11476, accessed 11 June 2009]; RSN Archive 116, fol. 7–7v.

333 Gervase Huxley, *Victorian Duke. The Life of Hugh Lupus Grosvenor, First Duke of Westminster* (Oxford University Press, London 1967); RSN Archive 164 School of Art Needlework Guarantee Fund (1874–1875); RSN Archive 119, fols 27 and 68; RSN Archive 117, fols 13 and 84; RSN Archive 79, fol. 17v; RSN Archive 83, fol. 63. Westminster acquired several embroideries worked at the School from designs by Crane, Burne-Jones, Jekyll and Lady Alford.

334 www.thepeerage.com/p1719.htm#i17184; *Memorandum and Articles of Association*, p. 16.

335 www.thepeerage.com/p2058.htm#i20575; Susan P Casteras and Colleen Denney, *The Grosvenor Gallery. A Palace of Art in Victorian England* (Yale University Press, New Haven and London, 1996), pp 1–37; *Memorandum and Articles of Association*, p. 16.

336 TNA, Census Returns for England 1851, HO107/1476 fol. 58 p. 23; *Proceedings of the Society of Antiquaries of London*, 2nd series, XIX (1901–1903), p. 106.

BIBLIOGRAPHY

Manuscripts

Private Collection
Welby papers
Stanway papers

Royal School of Needlework, Hampton Court Palace, Surrey (RSN)
RSN Archive 17 Admissions Register (1872–1922)
RSN Archive 79 Finance Committee Agenda Book (1881–1885)
RSN Archive 83 Managing Committee Minutes (1882–1885)
RSN Archive 109 Receipts and Payments (1876–77)
RSN Archive 116 Finance Committee Minutes (1878–1885)
RSN Archive 117 Managing Committee Minutes (1877–1882)
RSN Archive 119 Managing Committee Minutes (1875–1876)
RSN Archive 130 Case as Sent to Counsel for Opinion (1882); Montague Muir Mackenzie's 'Opinion' (1882); Assignment of Copyright of The Handbook of Embroidery (27 January 1883)
RSN Archive 136/5 Brochure for the School of Art Needlework ([October 1873])
RSN Archive 136/14 Catalogue of Embroideries ([March 1876])
RSN Archive 136/17 List of Classes in Ornamental Needlework (September 1877)
RSN Archive 136/18 Catalogue of the Special Exhibition of Needlework ([1877])
RSN Archive 136/21 Memorandum of Conditions to be subscribed by persons desirous of becoming agents of the Sale of Needlework of the School, 187[?]
RSN 136/22 List of Classes in Ornamental Needlework (September 1878)
RSN Archive 136/23 Finished Work ([1878])
RSN Archive 136/23a Prepared Work ([1878])
RSN Archive 136/26a Royal School of Art Needlework Prospectus (June 1879)
RSN Archive 136/30 Catalogue of the Glasgow Exhibition ([1879])
RSN Archive 136/32 Memorandum of Conditions to be subscribed by persons desirous of becoming agents of the Sale of Needlework of the School, (188[?])

RSN 136/33 Instructions for Teachers (February 1880)

RSN Archive 136/35 Prospectus for the Glasgow Branch of the RSN ([1880])

RSN Archive 136/43 Draft advertisement announcing the RSN's desire to execute ecclesiastical work from designs supplied to them by architects or artists for church decoration (May 1881)

RSN Archive 136/46 Advertising card with a list of agents in Britain and North America ([1881])

RSN Archive 136/69 Advertising Brochure ([1884])/ Price list for finished and prepared work ([1885])

RSN Archive 136/104 Royal School of Art Needlework Prospectus ([1892])

RSN Archive 164 School of Art Needlework Guarantee Fund (1874–1875); Brochure for the School of Art Needlework ([1874]); Brochure for the Royal School of Art Needlework ([c1908])

RSN Archive 210 Art Committee Minutes (1875–1883)

RSN Archive 216 School of Art Needlework Minute Book (1873–1875)

RSN Archive D1 Design Cards

RSN Archive D2 Book of Designs (c1872–1879)

RSN Archive D5 Box of Designs, late 19th–early 20th centuries

RSN Archive D6 Designs by Walter Crane for the Philadelphia International Centennial Exhibition (1875–1876)

Berkeley Castle, Glos

Berkeley GBB177 Steward's accounts (1870–1879)

Birmingham Museums and Art Gallery, Birmingham

Accession no. 1904P190 Edward Burne-Jones, *Poesis* (1873–1875)

Lincolnshire Archives, Lincoln (LA)

Brownlow personal papers, Diary of Lady Marian Alford (1875, 1877, 1883–1884)

Brownlow MS BNLW 4/8/2/6, Album containing reviews of Lady Marian Alford's *Needlework as Art* (1886)

Brownlow MS BNLW 2/2/7/11/ Furniture Ornamental Screens (1886)

The National Archives, Kew (TNA)

Census Returns for England and Wales (1851–1901)

Copy 1/652, Copyright Office Entry Forms (July–September 1882)

London Metropolitan Archives

St Pancras Parish Church, Register of Marriages, P90/PANL

Royal Institute of British Architects (RIBA)
SC127/1 Design for a counterpane for the Honourable Mrs Wyndham (May 1873)
SC 127/6 Design for a Portière (December 1875)

Kensington Central Library
Crane Portfolio F(1)/18 Sketch for a screen panel (nd)
Crane Portfolio G(6)/39 Rough designs for a screen (nd)

Printed Sources

Adburgham, Alison, *Shops and Shopping 1800–1914*, 2nd edn (Barrie & Jenkins, London, 1981)

Alford, Lady Marian, 'Art Needlework', *The Nineteenth Century*, 49 (March 1881), pp 439–49

Alford, Lady Marian, *Needlework as Art* (Sampson Low, Marston, Searle, and Rivington, London, 1886)

Anderson, Anne, 'A Golden Girl: Burne-Jones and Mary Stuart Wortley', *The Journal of William Morris Studies*, 13/1 (Autumn 1998), pp 64–71

Art Nouveau, Art Deco and Studio Pottery, Christies, 3 March 1981

Arts and Crafts Selling Exhibition, Liberty, Regent Street, London, June 2008

Beauman, Nicola, *Morgan: a Biography of E M Forster* (Hodder and Stoughton, London, 1993)

Beeton, Mrs Isabella, *Beeton's Book of Needlework* (Ward, Lock and Tyler, London, [1870])

Bertin-Guest, Josiane, *Chinese Embroidery: Traditional Techniques* (B T Batsford, London, 2003)

Brodie, Antonia, *et al* (eds), *Directory of British Architects*, II, 'L–Z' (Continuum, London and New York, 2001)

Brooke, Xanthe, *The Lady Lever Art Gallery Catalogue of Embroideries* (Alan Sutton Publishing Ltd, Stroud, 1992)

Burke, Doreen Bolger, *et al*, *In Pursuit of Beauty. Americans and the Aesthetics Movement* (Metropolitan Museum of Art, New York, 1986)

Burne-Jones, Lady Georgiana, *Memorials of Edward Burne-Jones*, 2 vols (The Macmillan Co, London & New York, 1904)

Callen, Anthea, *Angel in the Studio: Women in the Arts and Crafts Movement 1870–1914* (Astragal Books, London, 1979)

Casteras, Susan P and Denney, Colleen, *The Grosvenor Gallery. A Palace of Art in Victorian England* (Yale University Press, New Haven and London, 1996)

Catalogue of the Special Loan Exhibition of Decorative Art Needlework made before 1800 (Chiswick Press, London, 1874)

Caulfeild, S F A and Saward, Blanche C, *The Dictionary of Needlework*, 2 vols, 2nd edn (A W Cowan, London, 1887)

Cortazzi, Sir Hugh, *Britain and the 'Re-opening' of Japan: The Treaty of Yedo in 1858 and the Elgin Mission* (Japan Society Publications, London, 2008)

Costumes and Textiles 1500–1960, Sotheby's, 24 September 1980

Courbould, Elvina M, *Embroidery and Art Needlework Designs* (Hatchards, London, 1879)

Cox, Mabel, 'Arts and Crafts Workers II. Aldam Heaton', *The Artist* (March 1897), pp 121–27

Crane, Walter, *An Artist's Reminiscences* (Methuen & Co, London, 1907)

Daily News, 1878, 1880

Dakers, Caroline, *Clouds The Biography of a Country House* (Yale University Press, New Haven and London, 1993)

Dakers, Caroline, *The Holland Park Circle: Artists and Victorian Society* (Yale University Press, New Haven and London, 1999)

Davies, Martin, *Aldus Manutius Printer and Publisher of Renaissance Venice* (The British Library, London, 1995)

Dickinson, Donald C, *Dictionary of American Antique Bookdealers* (Westport, Connecticut & London, 1998)

DiGiulio, Katherine, *Natural Variations: Photographs by Colonel Stuart Wortley*, exhibition catalogue (Huntington Library, San Marino, California, 1994)

Dolby, Anastasia, *Church Embroidery Ancient and Modern* (Chapman and Hall, London, 1867)

Dolby, Anastasia, *Church Vestments: Their Origin, Use, and Ornament* (Chapman and Hall, London, 1868)

Donnelly, Max, 'Living with antiques. A collection of British art pottery and fin de siècle decorative arts', *The Magazine Antiques* (June 2008), pp 94–103

Dorinda's *Needlework for Ladies, for Pleasure and Profit* (London, 1883)

Edwards, Clive, *Encyclopedia of Furnishing Textiles, Floorcoverings and Home Furnishing Practices, 1200–1950* (Lund Humphries, Aldershot and Burlington, Vermont, 2007)

Fairclough, Oliver and Leary, Emmeline, *Textiles by William Morris and Morris & Co. 1861–1940* (Thames and Hudson, London, 1981)

Festing, Sally, *Gertrude Jekyll* (Penguin Books Ltd, London, 1991)

Garfield, Simon, *Mauve, How One Man Invented a Colour that Changed the World* (Faber & Faber, London, 2000)

Gaskell, Philip, *A New Introduction to Bibliography* (Oak Knoll Press, New Castle, Delaware, rep. 2007)

Glaister, Elizabeth, *Needlework* (MacMillan & Co, London, 1880)

Glasgow Herald, 1880

Guest, Revel and John, Angela V, *Lady Charlotte: A Biography of the Nineteenth Century* (Weidenfeld and Nicolson, London, 1989)

Hale, Lucretia Peabody (ed.), *Art Needlework for Decorative Embroidery*, 2nd edn (S W Tilton & Co, Boston, 1881)

Hand-book of Embroidery; Kensington Stitches Described and Illustrated. As Taught at the Royal School of Art-Needlework, at South Kensington, England (Perry Mason & Co, Boston, 1880, 1883)

Harper's Bazar, 1876, 1879, 1881

Harrison, Constance C, *Woman's Handiwork in Modern Homes* (Charles Scribner's Sons, New York, 1881)

Harvey, Charles and Press, Jon, 'The Businessman' in Linda Parry (ed.), *William Morris*, Victoria and Albert Museum exhibition catalogue (Philip Wilson Publishers Ltd, London, 1996), pp 49–57

Heaton, John Aldam, *Beauty and Art* (William Heinemann, London, 1897)

Hidden Burne-Jones: Works on Paper by Edward Burne-Jones from Birmingham Museums and Art Gallery, exhibition catalogue (Giles, London, 2007)

Higgin, Letitia, *Art as Applied to Dress* (Virtue & Co, London, 1885)

Huxley, Gervase, *Victorian Duke. The Life of Hugh Lupus Grosvenor, First Duke of Westminster* (Oxford University Press, London 1967)

International Health Exhibition. A Catalogue of Manufacturers, Decorations and Designs (London, 1881), 'National Scholars at Central School, South Kensington, 1863'

Jacques, Anne G, *Leek Embroidery* (Staffordshire Libraries, Arts and Archives, Stafford, 1990)

Jekyll, Francis, *Gertrude Jekyll A Memoir* (Jonathan Cape Ltd, London, 1934)

King, Brenda *Silk and Empire* (Manchester University Press, Manchester, 2005)

King, Brenda, *Dye, Print, Stitch: Textiles by Thomas and Elizabeth Wardle* (Published by the Author, Macclesfield, 2009)

Kramer, Elizabeth 'From specimen to scrap: Japanese textiles in the British Victorian interior, 1875–1900', in *Material Cultures, 1740–1920: The Meanings and Pleasures of Collecting* , eds John Potvin and Alla Myzelev (Ashgate Publishing Ltd, Farnham, 2009), pp 129–47

Kramer, Elizabeth, 'Japanese inspiration and the 'art' of Victorian art embroidery', *Text*, 37 (2009–10), pp 19–27

Lambert, Frances, *The Hand-book of Needlework* (John Murray, London and Wiley & Putnam, New York, 1842)

Lockwood, M S and Glaister, Elizabeth, *Art Embroidery: A Treatise on the Revived Practice of Decorative Needlework* (Marcus Ward & Co, London and Belfast, 1878)

Magazine of Art, 1880–1882, 1887

Marston, Edward, *After Work: Fragments from the Workshop of an Old Publisher* (William Heinemann and Charles Scribner's Sons, London and New York, 1904)

McKerrow, Ronald B, *An Introduction to Bibliography for Literary Students* (Oak Knoll Press, New Castle, Delaware, 1994)

McClaugherty, Martha Crabill, 'Household Art: Creating the Artistic Home, 1868–1893', *Winterthur Portfolio*, 18/1 (Spring 1983), pp 1–26

McLean, Ruari, *Joseph Cundall: a Victorian Publisher* (T A Constable Ltd, Edinburgh, 1976)

Memorandum and Articles of Association of the Royal School of Needlework (1878)

Morris, Barbara, *Victorian Embroidery* (Herbert Jenkins Ltd, London, 1962)

Morris, May, 'Opus Anglicanum – the Syon Cope', *Burlington Magazine*, 6 (1904–1905), pp 278–85

Myra's Journal of Dress and Fashion, 1880

Pall Mall Gazette, 1876, 1880

Padfield, Tim, *Copyright for Archivists and Records Managers*, 3rd edn (Facet Publishing, London, 2007)

Palliser, Mrs Bury, 'The School of Art Needlework', *The Art Journal*, 29 (1877), p. 213

Parry, Linda, *William Morris Textiles* (Weidenfeld and Nicholson Ltd, London, 1983)

Parry, Linda, 'Textiles', in Linda Parry (ed.), *William Morris*, Victoria and Albert Museum exhibition catalogue (Philip Wilson Publishers Ltd, London, 1996), pp 224–95

Parry, Linda, *Textiles of the Arts & Crafts Movement* (Thames and Hudson, London, 2005)

Paxman, Jeremy, *The Victorians: Britain Through the Paintings of the Age* (BBC Books, London, 2009)

Phillips, Patricia, 'The Queens Institute, Dublin (1861–1881)', in Norman McMillan (ed.), *Prometheus's Fire* (Tyndall Publications, Kilkenny, 2000)

Pine, Leslie Gilbert, *The New Extinct Peerage 1884–1971: Containing Extinct, Abeyant, Dormant and Suspended Peerages With Genealogies and Arms* (Heraldry Today, London, 1972)

Ponting, K G, *A Dictionary of Dyes and Dyeing* (Bell & Hyman, London, 1981)

Poulter, George C B, *The Courbould Genealogy* (Suffolk Institute of Archaeology, Ipswich, 1935)

Proceedings of the Society of Antiquaries of London, 2nd series, XIX (1901–1903)

Prospectus of the National Art Training School (HMSO, London, [185?–1895?])

Quilts, Costumes and Textiles, Christies, 16 April 1998

Rawson, George, 'The Arts and Crafts Movement and British Schools of Art', *The Decorative Arts Society Journal*, 28, 'Arts & Crafts Issue' (2004), pp 29–55

Reynolds, K D, *Aristocratic Women and Political Society in Victorian Britain* (Clarendon Press, Oxford, 1998)

Robbins, Daniel and Suleman, Reena, *Leighton House Museum* (The Royal Borough of Kensington and Chelsea, London, 2005)

Rock, Daniel, *Textile Fabrics; A Descriptive Catalogue Of the Collection of Church-vestments, Dresses, Silk Stuffs, Needlework and Tapestries, forming that Section of the [South Kensington] Museum* (Chapman and Hall, London, 1870)

Saint-Aubin, Charles Germain de, *Art of the Embroiderer* (1770), trans. Nikki Scheuer (Los Angeles County Museum of Art and David R Godine, Inc., Boston, Mass, 1983)

Schoeser, Mary, *English Church Embroidery 1833–1953*, 2nd edn (Watts & Co Ltd, London, 1998)

Smith, Walter, *Examples of Household Taste: The Industrial Art of the International Exhibition* (R Worthington, New York, [1877])

Spencer, Isobel, *Walter Crane* (MacMillan Publishing Co Inc, New York, 1975)

Stewart, J, 'Art Decoration: A Suitable Employment for Women', *The Art Journal*, 12 (1860), pp 70–71

Symondson SJ, Anthony, 'Art Needlework in Ireland', *Irish Arts Review*, 10 (1994), pp 126–35

Synge, Lanto, *Antique Needlework* (Blandford Press, London, rep. 1989)

Synge, Lanto, *Art of Embroidery: History, Style and Technique* (Antique Collectors' Club, Woodbridge, rep. 2006)

The Art Journal, 1886

The Atlantic Monthly, 1876, 1880

The Belfast News-Letter, 1877

The Best of British Design from the 19th and 20th Centuries, Sotheby's, 20 March 2008

The Graphic, 1880

The Ladies Field, 1889–1890

The Manchester Guardian, 1896

The Museums Area of South Kensington and Westminster, Survey of London, XXXVIII (The Athlone Press, University of London, London, 1975)

'The Needlework of Lady Carew and Mrs Clifford Cory', *Needlecraft* (Christmas 1906), pp 11–14, 25

The New York Times, 1880

The Scotsman, 1879–1880, 1885

The Sketch, 1895

The Telegraph, 1876

The Times, 1876, 1880, 1884, 1907

The Queen, 1874, 1876–1881

Tidman, Kathy Kajander, *Art for the Victorian Household* (Online Originals, London & Bordeaux, 1997)

Toomer, Heather, *Antique Lace* (Schiffer Publishing Ltd, Atglen, PA, 2001)

Townsend, W G Paulson, *Embroidery or The Craft of the Needle* (Truslove, Hanson & Comba Ltd, London and New York, 1899)

Tozer, Edward J F, *The South Devon Hunt* (Published by the Author, Teignmouth, 1916)

Travis, Anthony S, *The Colour Chemists* (London, Brent Schools and Industry Project, London, 1983)

Turner, Miss, *Practical Hints on the Revived Art of Crewel and Silk Embroidery* (M A Turner & Co, London, 1877)

Vallance, Aymer, 'The Royal School of Art Needlework', *The Magazine of Art*, 20 (1896–97), pp 243–48

Vice President's Report to H R H The President and The Council of The Royal School of Art Needlework for 1875 (London, 1876)

Walpole, E H, *Walpole Bros Ltd A Short History of the Firm* (Dublin, [1920])

Wheeler, Candace, *Yesterdays in a Busy Life* (Harper and Brothers, New York and London, 1918)

Wheeler, Candace, *The Development of Embroidery in America* (Harper and Bros, New York and London, 1921)

Wildman, Stephen and Christian, John, *Edward Burne-Jones Victorian Artist-Dreamer*, exhibition catalogue (Metropolitan Museum of Art, 1998)

Woman's Penny Paper, 1890

Wyllie, Diana, *The History of English Embroidery* (Diana Wyllie Ltd, London, nd), no.5 'Victorian and Modern Embroidery'

Yerburgh, E R, *Some Notes on our Family History* (Constable & Co Ltd, London, 1912)

Zakreski, Patricia, *Representing Female Artistic Labour 1848–1890: Refining Work for the Middle-Class Woman* (Ashgate, Aldershot, 2006)

Websites

www.bl.uk/collections/early/victorian/pu_intro.html, 'British Publishing 1800–1900', *Aspects of the Victorian Book*

www.britarch.ac.uk/lahs/tour/White%20Cross.htm, White Cross Mills

www.british-history.ac.uk/report.aspx?compid=22563, date accessed: 17 March 2009, 'Chiswick: Economic history', *A History of the County of Middlesex, 7, Acton, Chiswick, Ealing and Brentford, West Twyford, Willesden* (1982), pp 78–86

www.british-history.ac.uk/report.aspx?compid=41107, date accessed: 07 June 2008, 'St. Anne's Church', *Survey of London, 33–34, St Anne Soho* (1966), pp 256–77

www.british-history.ac.uk/report.aspx?compid=45926, date accessed: 7 May 2009, 'Rutland Gardens and South Place: Kent House and the Kent House Estate Development', *Survey of London, 45, Knightsbridge* (2000), pp 134–40

www.british-history.ac.uk/report.aspx?compid=53258, date accessed:
01 March 2009, 'Townships: Lancaster', *A History of the County of Lancaster*, 8 (1914), pp 33–48

www.collections.tepapa.govt.nz/search.aspx?term=Jane%20Cory

www.gilliat1.50megs.com/catalog.html, Descendants of John Gilliat,
Generation no. 2/4/19

www.hups.net/~lwuth/brangwin/2003_12_newsletter.html, David Brangwyn,
'William Curtis Brangwyn Architect and Church Embroidery Designer',
Brangwin Family Newsletter (December 2003)

http://.library.princeton.edu/libraries/firestone/rbsc/aids/scribner/, Charles
Scribner's Sons: An Illustrated Chronology

www.oxforddnb.com

www.oxfordmusiconline.com/subscriber/article/grove/music/24331?q=Sainton-
Dolby&search=quick&source=omo_gmo&pos=1&_start=1#firsthit

www.rootsweb.ancestry.com/cgi-bin/igm.cgi?op=AHN&db=:907399&id
=I0353, Shelley Lock family trees, Generation no. 1, Thomas Housman
Higgin

www.singletonsdiary.wordpress.com/2009/03/04/nugent-wade/,
'Nugent Wade', R C Singleton's Diary (1847): Diary of a Victorian
educational reformer

www.thepeerage.com

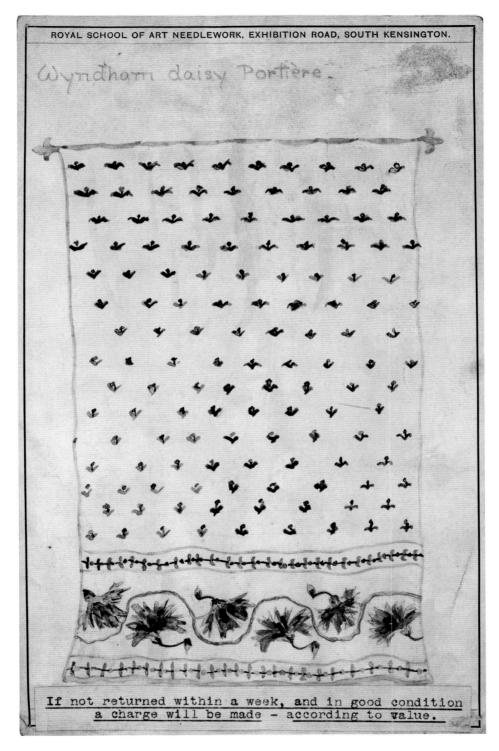

Fig. 2 Madeline Wyndham, Daisy Portière, undated.

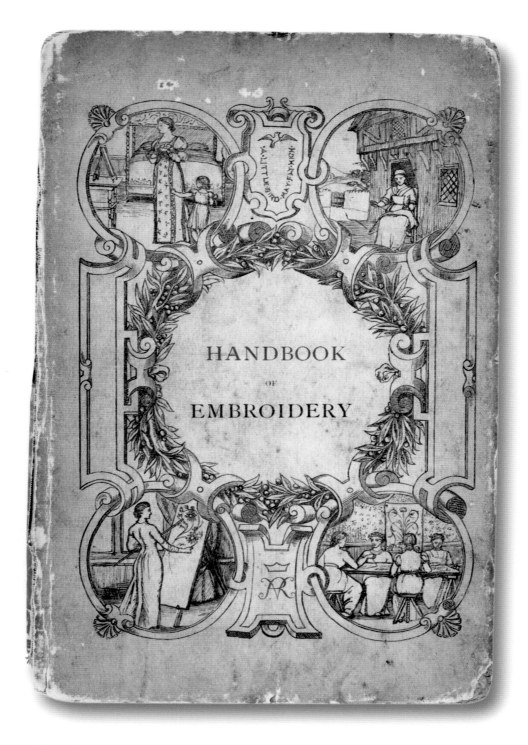

HANDBOOK

OF

EMBROIDERY

Fig. 3 Letitia Higgin, *Handbook of Embroidery* (London, 1880), cover 1.

84

Fig. 4
Letitia Higgin,
*Handbook of
Embroidery* (London,
1880), cover 2.

Fig. 5 Walter Crane, *Swan,
Rush and Iris* wallpaper
pattern, 1875.

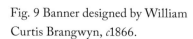

Design by the Rev. Selwyn Image, R.S.A. Needlework.

Fig. 7 Selwyn Image, *Juno*, photographed by Sampson Low and Co, *c*1879–1880.

Fig. 8 Thomas Wardle, *Strility*, 1884, detail.

Fig. 9 Banner designed by William Curtis Brangwyn, *c*1866.

Fig. 10 Syon cope,
English, 1300–1320,
detail.

Fig. 11 Embroidery
frame from Anastasia
Dolby, *Church
Embroidery Ancient
and Modern* (London,
1867), plate 18.

Fig. 12 RSN workroom, Exhibition Road, *c*1903.

Fig. 13 Christiana Cresswell, *Vine* curtain, mid–1870s.

Fig. 14
Three-panel
Oriental
screen,
designed and
embroidered
by Mary
Gemmell,
c1876.

Fig. 15 Selwyn
Image, Cushion
cover, designed for
the prepared work
department of the
RSN, 1880s, detail.

89

Figs 16a–b Designs supplied by the Royal School of Art Needlework, supplement to *The Queen*, 16 July 1881 and 11 February 1882.

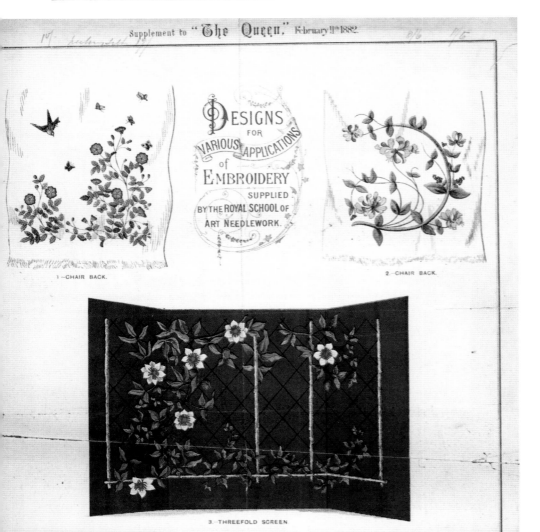

Fig. 17 *Hand–Book of Embroidery*
(Boston 1883).

Fig. 18
Edward Burne-
Jones, *Musica*,
embroidered by the
RSN, undated.

92

Fig. 19
Edward Burne-
Jones, *Poesis*,
embroidered by
the RSN, 1880.

Fig. 20 Walter
Crane, *Complete
Design for
Decorating a
Room with
Hangings*,
1875–1876.

Figs 21a–b
Walter Crane,
preparatory
designs for the
Elements screen,
late 1870s.

Fig. 22 Walter Crane, *Elements* screen, embroidered by the RSN, *c*1879.

Figs 23a–b Pair of panels based on Walter Crane's design for the *Elements* screen, probably embroidered by the RSN in the late 1870s.

95

Figs 24a–b Walter Crane, *Daffodil* and *Primrose*, c1876.

Fig. 25 George Aitchison, Floral design 'embroidered on blue satin', 7 October 1876.

Fig. 27 Fairfax B Wade, *Forget-me-not* design, November 1874.

Fig. 28 Hanging stitched by
Lady Emily Plowden,
undated, detail.

Figs 29a–b Selwyn Image, *Juno* and
Minerva, embroidered by the RSN, *c*1879.

Fig. 30 Selwyn Image, *Venus*,
embroidered by the RSN, undated.

Fig. 31 Helen Marion
Burnside, Magnolia, undated.

HANDBOOK OF EMBROIDERY.

HANDBOOK OF EMBROIDERY

BY L. HIGGIN.

EDITED BY LADY MARIAN ALFORD.

PUBLISHED BY AUTHORITY OF THE ROYAL SCHOOL OF ART
NEEDLEWORK, AND DEDICATED TO THEIR
PRESIDENT,

H.R.H. PRINCESS CHRISTIAN, OF SCHLESWIG-
HOLSTEIN, PRINCESS OF GREAT BRITAIN
AND IRELAND.

LONDON:

SAMPSON LOW, MARSTON, SEARLE, AND RIVINGTON,

CROWN BUILDINGS, FLEET STREET.

1880.

NOTE.

Plates Nos. 4 and 19 show a portion only of the designs by Mr. W. Morris and Mr. Fairfax Wade.

PREFACE.

IN drawing up this little "Handbook of Embroidery" we do not pretend to give such complete technical directions as would enable a beginner in this beautiful art to teach herself; because learning without practical lessons must be incomplete, and can only lead to disappointment.

We have sought, therefore, only to respond to the inquiries we are constantly receiving, and to supply useful hints to those who are unable to avail themselves of lessons, and are forced to puzzle over their difficulties without help from a trained and experienced embroiderer; at the same time, the rules we have laid down and the directions we have given may serve to remind those who have passed through the classes, of many little details which might easily be forgotten when the lessons are over, though so much of the success of embroidery depends upon them.

We have given a short description of the most useful
stitches, and have pointed out their applicability to different styles of work ; we have named the various materials which are best suited as grounds for embroidery,
and the silks, filoselles, crewels, &c., which are most commonly employed, with practical rules for their use in the
best and most economical manner.

Also we have given such plain directions as to stretching, framing, and cleaning the work as are possible in a
limited space, and without practical illustration. We
venture to hope we have thus supplied a want that has
been long felt by those who interest themselves in the
art in which Englishwomen once excelled, but which had
languished of late years, and almost died out amongst
us, though it has always been taught in many continental
cities, where embroideries have never ceased to be required for church decoration.

We have abstained from giving any directions as to
the tracing of designs upon material, for two sufficient
reasons : firstly, that the Royal School of Art-Needlework has never supplied designs alone, or in any other
form than as prepared work ; and secondly, that having
made experiments with all the systems that have been
brought out for "stamping," ironing from transfer-papers,
or with tracing powder, it has been found that designs
can only be artistically and well traced on material by
hand painting. Those ladies who can design and paint
their own patterns for embroidery are independent of
assistance, and to those who are unable to do so we
cannot recommend any of the methods now advertised.

It has been thought unnecessary to enter into the subject of ecclesiastical embroidery at present. This has been so thoroughly revived in England, and practised in such perfection by sisterhoods—both Anglican and Roman Catholic—as well as by some of the leading firms of church decorators, that we have not felt ourselves called upon to do more than include it in our course of lessons.

The æsthetic side of our subject we have purposely avoided, as it would lead us further than this purely technical guide-book pretends to go. But we propose shortly to bring out a second part devoted to design, composition, colour, and the common-sense mode of treating decorative Art, as applied to wall-hanging, furniture, dress, and the smaller objects of luxury.

We shall examine and try to define the principles which have guided Eastern and Western embroideries at their best periods, hoping thus to save the designers of the future from repeating exploded experiments against received canons of good taste ; checking, if we can, the exuberance of ignorant or eccentric genius, but leaving room for originality.

Mrs. Dolby, who by her presence and her teaching helped Lady Welby to start the Royal School of Art-Needlework, has left behind her a most valuable guide for mediæval work in her " Church Embroidery, Ancient and Modern," which will always be a first-class authority.

The Author and the Editor of this handbook are equally impressed with the responsibility they have undertaken in formulating rules for future embroiderers. They have consulted all acknowledged authorities, and from them have selected those which the teachers in the Royal School of Art-Needlework have found the most practical and instructive.

Should any of their readers favour them with hints or criticisms, or give them information as to pieces of embroidery worth studying, or stitches not here named, any such communications will be gratefully received and made use of in future editions.

THE EDITOR.

TABLE OF CONTENTS.

CHAPTER I.

Page 1.

OF IMPLEMENTS AND MATERIALS USED IN MODERN EMBROIDERY.

CHAPTER II.

Page 11.

TEXTILE FABRICS USED AS GROUNDS FOR EMBROIDERY.

CHAPTER III.

Page 19.

STITCHES.

CHAPTER IV.

Page 33.

CHAPTER V.

Page 37.

STITCHES USED IN FRAME EMBROIDERY.

CONTENTS.

ILLUSTRATIONS.

HANDBOOK OF EMBROIDERY.

CHAPTER I.

OF MATERIALS AND IMPLEMENTS USED IN MODERN EMBROIDERY.

IMPLEMENTS.

Needles.—The best "embroidery needles" for ordinary crewel hand-work are Nos. 5 and 6. For coarse "sail-cloth," "flax," or "oatcake," No. 4. For frame embroidery, or very fine hand-work, the higher numbers, from 7 to 10.

It is a mistake to use too fine a needle. The thread of crewel or silk should always be able to pass loosely into the eye, so as not to require any pulling to carry it through the material.

Scissors should be finely pointed, and very sharp.

Thimbles which have been well worn, and are therefore smooth, are best.   Some workers prefer ivory or vulcanite.   Two thimbles should be used for frame-work.

Prickers are necessary for piercing holes in gold embroidery, and also for arranging the lie of the thread in some forms of couching.

MATERIALS.

CREWELS, AND HOW TO USE THEM.

Crewel should be cut into short threads, never more than half the length of the skein. If a long needleful is used, it is not only apt to pull the work, but is very wasteful, as the end of it is liable to become frayed or knotted before it is nearly worked up. If it is necessary to use it double (and for coarse work, such as screen panels on sailcloth, or for embroidering on Utrecht velvet, it is generally better doubled), care should be taken never to pass it through the eye of the needle, knotting the two ends; but two separate threads of the length required should be passed together through the needle.

Crewel should not be manufactured with a twist, as it makes the embroidery appear hard and rigid; and the shades of colour do not blend into each other so harmoniously as when they are untwisted.

In crewels of the best quality the colours are perfectly fast, and will bear being repeatedly washed, provided no soda or washing-powder is used. Directions for cleaning crewel work are given later; but it should not be sent to an ordinary laundress, who will most certainly ruin the colours.

Crewel is suitable for embroidery on all kinds of linen —on plain or diagonal cloth, serge, flannel, &c. It is also very effective when used in conjunction with embroidery silk, or filoselle, either in conventional designs, or where flowers are introduced. The leaves may be worked in crewels, and the flowers in silk, or the effect of the crewels increased by merely touching up the high lights with silk.

Tapestry Wool is more than twice the thickness of crewel, and is used for screen panels, or large curtain borders, where the work is coarse, and a good deal of ground has to be covered. It is also used for bath blankets and carriage and sofa rugs. Tapestry wool is not yet made in all shades.

Fine crewels are used for delicately working small figures, d'oyleys, &c.; but there is also a difficulty about obtaining these in all shades, as there is not much demand for them at present.

Arrasene is a new material. It is a species of worsted chenille, but is not twisted round fine wire or silk, like ordinary chenille; though it is woven first into a fabric, and then cut in the same manner. It serves to produce broad effects for screen panels, or borders, and has a very soft, rich appearance when carefully used. It is made also in silk; but this is inferior to worsted arrasene, or the old-fashioned chenille.

SILKS.

"*Embroidery," or Bobbin Silk*, which has now almost superseded floss, is used for working on satin and silk, or for any fine work. It is made in strands, each of which has a slight twist in it to prevent its fraying as floss does. As this silk is required in all varieties of thickness, it is manufactured in what is technically called "rope," that is, with about twelve strands in each thread. When not "rope" silk, it is in single strands, and is then called "fine" silk. As it is almost always necessary to use several strands, and these in varying number, according to the embroidery in hand, the rope silk has to be divided, or the fine doubled or trebled, as the case may be.

If rope silk is being used, the length required for a needleful must be cut and passed carefully between finger and thumb once or twice, that it may not be twisted. It should then be carefully separated into the number of strands most suitable for the embroidery in hand ; for ordinary work three is about the best number.

These must be threaded together through the needle, care being taken not to tangle the piece of "rope" from which they have been detached. There need be no waste if this operation is carefully done, as good silk will always divide into strands without fraying.

In using " fine silk," one length must be cut first, then other strands laid on it,—as many as are needed to form the thickness required.   They should be carefully laid in the same direction as they leave the reel or card.   If placed carelessly backwards and forwards, they are sure to fray, and will not work evenly together.   With silk still more than with crewel, it is necessary to thread all the strands through the needle together, never to double one back, and never to make a knot.

It is intended in future to do away with this distinction between "rope" and "fine" silk, and to have it all manufactured of one uniform thickness, which will consist of eight strands of the same quality as the "fine" silk at present in use.   As it will, however, still be necessary to divide the thread, and even perhaps occasionally to double it, the directions given above will be useful.

Purse Silk is used sometimes for diapering, and in rare cases in ordinary embroidery, where a raised effect is required.

Raw or *spun silk* is a soft untwisted cream-coloured silk, used for daisies and other simple white flowers, or in outlining.   It is much cheaper than embroidery silk or filoselle.

Vegetable Silk (so-called) is not used or sold by the Royal School.

Filoselle, when of good quality, is not, as some people suppose, a mixture of silk and cotton. It is pure silk, but of an inferior quality; and therefore cheaper. It answers many of the purposes of bobbin silk; but is not suitable for fine embroidery on silk or satin fabrics. It should be used also in strands, and the same remarks hold good with regard to its not being doubled, but cut in equal lengths.

Tussore.—Interesting experiments have recently been made with the "Tussore," or "wild silk" of India, which bids fair to create a revolution in embroidery. Not only can it be produced for less than half the price of the "cultivated silk" of Italy, China, or Japan, but it also takes the most delicate dyes with a softness that gives a peculiarly charming effect. It can scarcely be said to be in the market as yet, but in all probability before this work is through the press it will have become an important element in decorative needlework. It is much less glossy than cultivated silk.

GOLD THREAD, &c.

"*Japanese gold thread,*" which has the advantage of never tarnishing, is now extremely difficult to obtain. Being made of gilt paper twisted round cotton thread, it cannot be drawn through the material by the needle; but must in all cases be laid on, and stitched down with a fine yellow silk, known as "Maltese," or "Horse-tail."

"*Chinese gold*" is manufactured in the same manner as the Japanese; but being of a much redder colour is not so satisfactory in embroidery unless a warm shade is desirable for a particular work.

Gold and silver passing, a very fine kind of thread, can either be used for working through the material, or can be laid on like the Japanese gold. They are suitable for "raised gold or silver embroidery."

Bullion, or Purl, is gold or silver wire made in a series of continuous rings, like a corkscrew. It is used in ecclesiastical work, for embroidering official and military uniforms, and for heraldic designs. It should be cut into the required lengths—threaded on the needle and fastened down as in bead-work. Purl is sometimes manufactured with a coloured silk twisted round the metal though not concealing it, and giving rich tints to the work.

Spangles were anciently much used in embroidery, and were sometimes of pure gold. They are but little used now.

Plate consists of narrow plates of gold or silver stitched on to the embroidery by threads of silk, which pass over them.

The French and English gold thread is made of thin plates of metal cut into strips, and wound round strands of cotton in the same manner as the Japanese gold. If the metal is real, the cost is of course great. It is sold by weight, gold being about 20s. per oz., and silver, 10s. per oz. In addition to its superiority in wear, it has this advantage, that old gold or silver thread is always of intrinsic value, and may be sold at the current price of the metal whatever state it may be in. Many varieties of gilt thread are manufactured in France and England, which may be used when the great expense of "real gold" is objected to. But although it looks equally well at first, it soon becomes tarnished, and spoils the effect of the embroidery. Gold and silver threads are difficult to work with in England, and especially in London, as damp and coal-smoke tarnish them almost before the work is out of the frame. Mrs. Dolby recommends cloves being placed in the papers in which they are kept.

RECIPES FOR PRESERVING GOLD.

WE give here two recipes, which may be found serviceable. They are from different sources; the first is a very old one. They may preserve gold for a certain time.

1. Isinglass dissolved in spirits of wine and brushed over the thread or braid, which should be hung over something to dry, and not touched with the hand.

2. Spirits of wine and mastic varnish mixed very thin and put on in the same way with a brush.

CHAPTER II.

TEXTILE FABRICS USED AS GROUNDS FOR
EMBROIDERY.

LINENS.

THERE are many varieties of unglazed, half-bleached linens, from that thirty-six and forty inches wide, used for chair-back covers, to that ninety inches wide, used for large table-covers, curtains, &c. There are also endless varieties of fancy linens, both of hand and power-loom weaving, for summer dresses, for bed furniture, chair-back covers, table-cloths, &c.

Flax is the unbleached brown linen, often used for chair-back covers.

Twill is a thick linen suitable for coverings for furniture.

Kirriemuir Twill is a fine twilled linen made at Kirriemuir, and is good for tennis aprons, dresses, curtains, &c.

Sailcloth is a stout linen, of yellow colour, and is only suitable for screen panels.

Oatcake Linen, so called from its resemblance to Scotch oatcake, has been popular for screen panels or wash-stand backs.   It is very coarse and rough.

Oatmeal Linen is finer and of a greyer tone.   It is also used for screens, and for smaller articles.

Smock Linen is a strong even green cloth.   It makes an excellent ground for working screens, and is also used for tennis aprons.

Crash.—Properly speaking, the name "*crash*" is only applied to the coarse Russian home-spun linen, which has been such a favourite from the beauty of its tone of colour.   It is, however, erroneously applied to all linens used for embroidery, whether woven by hand-loom or machinery ; and this confusion of names frequently leads to mistakes.   Crash is almost always very coarse, is never more than eighteen inches wide, and cannot be mistaken for a machine-made fabric.   It is woven by the Russian peasants in their own homes, in lengths varying from five to ten yards, and, therefore, though sent over in large bales, it is very difficult to find two pieces among a hundred that in any way match each other.

Bolton, or Workhouse Sheeting, is a coarse twilled cotton fabric, seventy-two inches wide, of a beautiful soft creamy colour, which improves much in washing.   It is inexpensive, and an excellent ground for embroidery, either for curtains, counterpanes, chair coverings, or for ladies' dresses, or tennis aprons.

It resembles the twilled cotton on which so much of the old crewel embroidery was worked in the seventeenth century, and is one of the most satisfactory materials when of really good quality.

All descriptions of linen, except the "oatcake" and "sailcloth," can be embroidered in the hand.

TEXTILE FABRICS.

SATINS AND SILKS.

Satins and Silks can only be embroidered in a frame. Furniture satins of stout make, with cotton backs, may be used without backing; but ordinary dress satins require to have a thin cotton or linen backing to bear the strains of the work and framing. Nothing is more beautiful than a rich white satin for a dress embroidered in coloured silks.

For fans, a very fine, closely woven satin is necessary, as it will not fold evenly unless the satin is thin; and yet it must be rich enough to sustain the fine embroidery, without pulling, or looking poor. A special kind of satin is made for the manufacture of fans, and none other is available.

"*Silk Sheeting*" of good quality, "*Satin de Chine*," and other silk-faced materials of the same class, may either be embroidered in the hand, or framed; but for large pieces of work a frame is essential. These materials are suitable for curtains, counterpanes, piano coverings, or panels, and indeed for almost any purpose. The finer qualities are very beautiful for dresses, as they take rich and graceful folds, and carry embroidery well.

Tussore and Corah Silks are charming for summer dresses, light chair-back covers, or embroidered window blinds. They will only bear light embroidering in silk or filoselle.

Within the last year successful experiments have been made in dyeing these Indian silks in England. The exact shades which we admire so much in the old Oriental embroideries have been reproduced, with the additional advantage of being perfectly fast in colour.

Nothing can be more charming as lining for table covers, screens, curtains, &c.; and they are rather less expensive than other lining silks.

The fabrics known as *Plain Tapestries* are a mixture of silk and cotton, manufactured in imitation of the hand-worked backgrounds so frequent in ancient embroideries—especially Venetian. Almost all the varieties of *Opus Pulvinarium*, or cushion stitch, have been reproduced in these woven fabrics.

Brocatine is a silk-faced material, woven to imitate couched embroidery. The silk is thrown to the surface and is tied with cotton threads from the back.

As grounds for embroidery it has an excellent effect.

TEXTILE FABRICS.

COTTONS AND WOOLLENS.

Velveteen, if of good quality, makes an excellent ground for screen panels, chair-covers, portières, curtains, borders, &c. It can be worked in the hand if the embroidery be not too heavy or large in style.

Utrecht Velvet is only suitable for coarse crewel or tapestry wool embroidery. It is fit for curtain dados or wide borderings.

Velvet Cloth is a rich plain cloth, finished without any gloss. It is a good ground for embroidery, either for curtains or altar-cloths. It is two yards wide.

Felt is sometimes used for the same purposes, but does not wear nearly so well, and is difficult to work.

Diagonal Cloth can be worked either in the hand or frame, although it is always much better in the latter. It is used for table-covers, curtains, chair-seats, &c.

Serge is usually made thirty-six inches wide. It has long been in favour for curtains, small table-covers, dresses, &c. It can now be obtained at the school fifty-four inches wide, in many shades.

Soft or Super Serge, also fifty-four inches wide, is an excellent material, much superior in appearance to diagonal cloth, or to the ordinary rough serge. It takes embroidery well.

Cricketing flannel is used for coverlets for cots, children's dresses, and many other purposes. It is of a beautiful creamy colour, and is a good ground for fine crewel or silk embroidery. It need not be worked in a frame.

Genoa or Lyons Velvet makes a beautiful ground for embroidery; but it can only be worked in a frame, and requires to be " backed " with a thin cotton or linen lining, if it is to sustain any mass of embroidery. For small articles, such as sachets or casket-covers, when the work is fine and small, the backing is not necessary. Screen panels of velvet, worked wholly in crewels, or with crewel brightened with silk, are very effective. Three-piled velvet is the best for working upon, but is so expensive that it is seldom asked for.

Silk Velvet Plush (a new material) can only be used in frame work, and must be backed. It is useful in " appliqué " from the many beautiful tones of colour it takes. As a ground for silk or gold embroidery it is also very good.

C

TEXTILE FABRICS.

GOLD AND SILVER CLOTH.

Cloth of Gold or Silver is made of threads of silk woven with metal, which is thrown to the surface. In its best form it is extremely expensive, varying from £4 to £6 per yard, according to the weight of gold introduced. Cloth of silver is generally £3 the yard.

Inferior kinds of these cloths are made in which silk largely predominates, and shows plainly on the surface. They are frequently woven in patterns, such as diaper or diagonal lines, with a tie of red silk, in imitation of the diaper patterns of couched embroidery.

They are chiefly used in ecclesiastical or heraldic embroidery; their great expense preventing their general use.

CHAPTER III.

STITCHES USED IN HAND EMBROIDERY AS TAUGHT AT THE ROYAL SCHOOL OF ART-NEEDLEWORK.

To avoid pulling or puckering the work, care should be taken—firstly, that the needle is not too small, so as to require any force in drawing it through the material ; secondly, the material must be held in a convex position over the fingers, so that the crewel or silk in the needle shall be looser than the ground ; and thirdly, not to use too long needlefuls. These rules apply generally to all handworked embroideries.

STITCHES.

Stem Stitch.—The first stitch which is taught to a beginner is "stem stitch" (wrongly called also, "crewel stitch," as it has no claim to being used exclusively in crewel embroidery). It is most useful in work done in the hand, and especially in outlines of flowers, unshaded leaves, and arabesque, and all conventional designs.

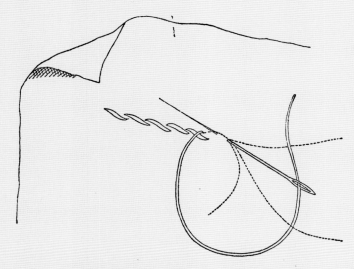

Illustration, No. 1.—STEM STITCH.

It may be best described as a long stitch forward on the surface, and a shorter one backward on the under side of the fabric, the stitches following each other almost in line from left to right. The effect on the wrong side is exactly that of an irregular back-stitching used by dressmakers, as distinguished from regular stitching. A leaf worked in outline should be begun at the lower or stalk end, and worked round the right side to the top, taking care that the needle is to the left of the thread as it is drawn out. When the point of the leaf is reached, it is best to reverse the operation in working down the left side towards the stalk again, so as to keep the needle to the right of the thread instead of to the left, as in going up.

The reason of this will be easily understood : we will suppose the leaf to have a slightly serrated edge (and

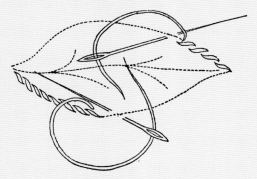

Illustration, No. 2.

there is no leaf in nature with an absolutely smooth one). It will be found that in order to give this ragged appearance, it is necessary to have the points at which the insertions of the needle occur on the outside of the leaf : whereas if the stem stitch were continued down the left side, exactly in the same manner as in ascending the right, we should have the ugly anomaly of a leaf outlined thus :—

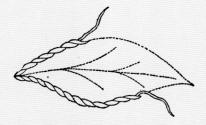

Illustration, No. 3.

If the leaf is to be worked "solidly," another row of stem stitching must be taken up the centre of it (unless it be a very narrow leaf), to the top. The two halves of the leaf must then be filled in, separately, with close, even rows of stem stitch, worked in the ordinary way,

with the needle to the left of the thread. This will prevent the ugly ridge which remains in the centre, if it is
worked round and round the inside of the outline. Stem
stitch must be varied according to the work in hand. If
a perfectly even line is required, care must be taken that
the direction of the needle when inserted is in a straight
line with the preceding stitch. If a slight serrature is
required, each stitch must be sloped a little by inserting
the needle at a slight angle, as shown in the illustration.

The length of the surface stitches must vary to suit
the style of each piece of embroidery.

Split Stitch is worked like ordinary "stem," except
that the needle is always brought up *through* the crewel
or silk, which it splits, in passing.

The effect is to produce a more even line than is
possible with the most careful stem stitch. It is used for

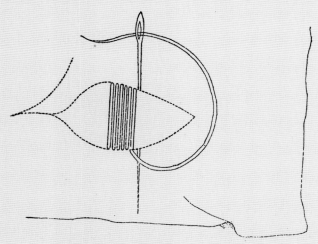

Illustration, No. 4.—SATIN STITCH.

delicate outlines. Split stitch is rarely used in hand
embroidery, being more suitable for frame work: but

has been described here as being a form of stem stitch. The effect is somewhat like a confused chain stitch.

Satin Stitch—French Plumetis—is one of those chiefly used in white embroidery, and consists in taking the needle each time back again almost to the spot from which it started, so that the same amount of crewel or silk remains on the back of the work as on the front. This produces a surface as smooth as satin: hence its name. It is chiefly used in working the petals of small flowers, such as "Forget-me-nots," and in arabesque designs where a raised effect is wanted in small masses.

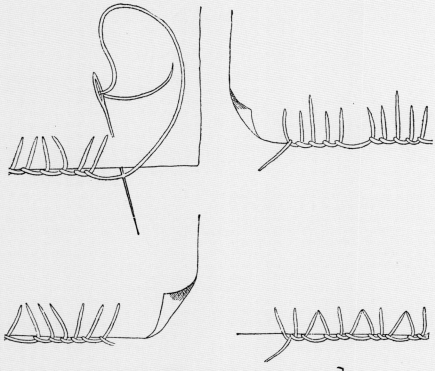

Illustration, No. 5.—BLANKET STITCH.]

Blanket Stitch is used for working the edges of table-covers, mantel valances, blankets, &c., or for edging any other material. It is simply a button-hole stitch, and may be varied in many ways by sloping the stitches alternately to right and left ; by working two or three together, and leaving a space between them and the next set ; or by working a second row round the edge of the cloth over the first with a different shade of wool.

Knotted Stitch, or *French Knot*, is used for the centres of such flowers as the daisy or wild rose, and sometimes for the anthers of others. The needle is brought up at

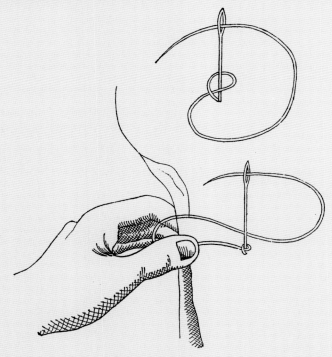

Illustration, No. 6.—KNOTTED STITCH, or FRENCH KNOT.

the exact spot where the knot is to be : the thread is held in the left hand, and twisted once or twice round the needle, the point of which is then passed through the fabric close to the spot where it came up: the right hand draws it underneath, while the thumb of the left keeps the thread in its place until the knot is secure. The knots are increased in size according to the number of twists round the needle. When properly made, they should look like beads, and lie in perfectly even and regular rows.

This stitch is very ancient, and does not seem confined to any country, and the Chinese execute large and elaborate pieces of embroidery in it, introducing beautiful shading. A curious specimen of very fine knotting stitch was exhibited at the Royal School in 1878, probably of French workmanship. It was a portrait of St. Ignatius Loyola, not more than six inches in length, and was entirely executed in knots of such fineness, that without a magnifying glass it was impossible to discover the stitches. This, however, is a *tour de force*, and not quoted as worthy of imitation.

There is one variety of this stitch, in which the thread is twisted a great many times round the needle, so as to form a sort of curl instead of a single knot. This is found in many ancient embroideries, where it is used for the hair of saints and angels in ecclesiastical work.

Knotted stitch was also employed largely in all its forms in the curious and ingenious but ugly style in vogue during the reign of James I., when the landscapes were frequently worked in cross, or feather stitch, while the figures were raised over stuffing, and dressed, as it were, in robes made entirely in point lace, or button-hole stitches, executed in silk. The foliage of the trees and shrubs which we generally find in these embroidered pictures, as well as the hair in the figures, were worked in knotted stitches of varying sizes, while the faces were in tent stitch or painted on white silk, and fastened on to the canvas or linen ground.

Another variety of knotting, which is still occasionally used, resembles *bullion*, being made into a long roll.

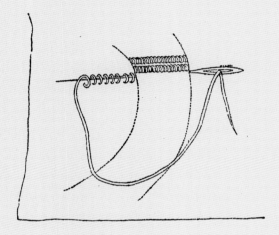

Illustration, No. 7.—BULLION KNOT.

A stitch of the length of the intended roll is taken in the material, the point of the needle being brought to the surface again in the same spot from which the thread originally started; the thread is then twisted eight or ten times round the point of the needle, which is drawn out carefully through the tunnel formed by the twists, this being kept in its place by the left thumb. The point of the needle is then inserted once more in the same place as it first entered the material, the long knot or roll being drawn so as to lie evenly between the points of insertion and re-appearance, thus treating the twisted thread as if it were bullion or purl.

Chain Stitch is but little used in embroidery now, although it may sometimes be suitable for lines. It is made by taking a stitch from right to left, and before the

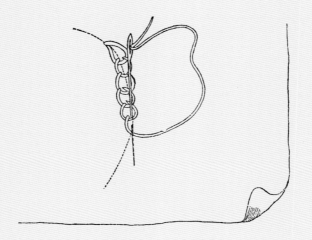

Illustration, No. 8.—CHAIN STITCH.

needle is drawn out the thread is brought round towards the worker, and under the point of the needle.

The next stitch is taken from the point of the loop thus formed forwards, and the thread again kept under the point, so that a regular chain is formed on the surface of the material.

This chain stitch was much employed for ground patterns in the beautiful gold-coloured work on linen for dress or furniture which prevailed from the time of James I. to the middle of the eighteenth century. It gave the appearance of quilting when worked on linen in geometrical designs, or in fine and often-repeated arabesques. Examples of it come to us from Germany and Spain, in which the design is embroidered in satin stitch, or entirely filled in with solid chain stitch, in a uniform gold colour.

Chain stitch resembles *Tambour work*, which we shall describe amongst framework stitches, though it is not at present practised at this School.

Twisted Chain, or Rope stitch.

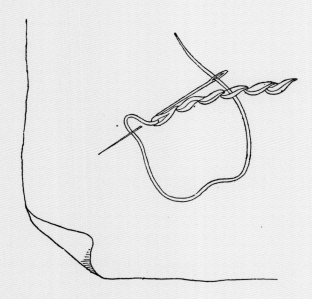

Illustration, No. 9.—TWISTED CHAIN.

Effective for outlines on coarse materials, such as blankets, carriage rugs, footstools, &c.

It is like an ordinary chain, except that in place of starting the second stitch from the centre of the loop, the needle is taken back to half the distance behind it, and the loop is pushed to one side to allow the needle to enter in a straight line with the former stitch. It is not of much use, except when worked with double crewel or with tapestry wool ; and should then have the appearance of a twisted rope.

Feather Stitch.—Vulgarly called "*long and short stitch,*" "*long stitch,*" and sometimes "*embroidery stitch.*" We propose to restore to it its ancient title of feather stitch— "*Opus Plumarium,*" so called from its supposed resemblance to the plumage of a bird.

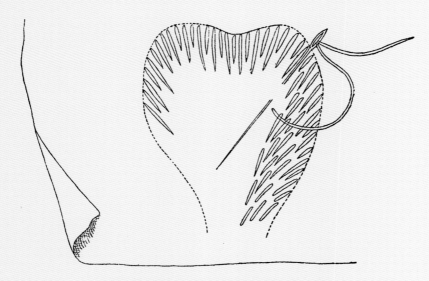

Illustration, No. 10.—FEATHER STITCH.

We shall now describe it as used for handwork ; and later (at page 37), as worked in a frame. These two modes differ very little in appearance, as the principle is the same, namely, that the stitches are of varying length, and are worked into and between each other, adapting themselves to the form of the design, but in handwork the needle is kept on the surface of the material.

Feather Stitch is generally used for embroidering flowers, whether natural or conventional.

In working the petal of a flower (such as we have chosen for our illustration), the outer part is first worked in with stitches which form a close, even edge on the outline, but a broken one towards the centre of the petal, being alternately long and short. These edging stitches resemble satin stitch in so far that the same amount of crewel or silk appears on the under, as on the upper side of the work : they must slope towards the narrow part of the petal.

The next stitches are somewhat like an irregular "stem," inasmuch as they are longer on the surface than on the under side, and are worked in between the uneven lengths of the edging stitches so as to blend with them. The petal is then filled up by other stitches, which start from the centre, and are carried between those already worked.

When the petal is finished, the rows of stitches should be so merged in each other that they cannot be distinguished, and when shading is used, the colours should appear to melt into each other.

In serrated leaves, such as hawthorn or virginia creeper, the edging stitches follow the broken outline of the leaf instead of forming an even outer edge.

It is necessary to master thoroughly this most important stitch, but practice only can make the worker perfect.

The work should always be started by running the thread a little way in front of the embroidery. Knots should never be used except in rare cases, when it is impossible to avoid them. The thread should always be finished off on the surface of the work, never at the back, where there should be no needless waste of material. No untidy ends or knots should ever appear there; in fact, the wrong side should be quite as neat as the right. It is a mistake to suppose that pasting will ever do away with the evil effects of careless work, or will steady embroidery which has been commenced with knots, and finished with loose ends at the back.

The stitches vary constantly according to their application, and good embroiderers differ in their manner of using them: some preferring to carry the thread back towards the centre of the petal, on the surface of the work, so as to avoid waste of material; others making their stitches as in satin stitch—the same on both sides, but these details may be left to the intelligence and taste of the worker, who should never be afraid of trying experiments, or working out new ideas.

Nor should she ever fear to unpick her work; for only by experiment can she succeed in finding the best combinations, and one little piece ill done, will be sufficient to spoil her whole embroidery, as no touching-up can afterwards improve it.

We have now named the principal stitches used in hand-embroidery, whether to be executed in crewel or silk.

There are, however, numberless other stitches used in crewel embroidery: such as ordinary stitching, like that used in plain needlework, in which many designs were formerly traced on quilted backgrounds—others, again, are many of them lace stitches, or forms of herringbone, and are used for filling in the foliage of large conventional floriated designs, such as we are accustomed to see in the English crewel work of the sixteenth and seventeenth centuries, on a twilled cotton material, resembling our modern Bolton sheeting.

It would be impossible to describe or even enumerate them all ; as varieties may be constantly invented by an ingenious worker to enrich her design, and in lace work there are already 100 named stitches, which occasionally are used in decorative embroidery. Most of these, if required, can be shown as taught at the Royal School of Art-Needlework, and are illustrated by samplers.

CHAPTER IV.

FRAMES AND FRAMING.

BEFORE proceeding to describe the various stitches used in frame embroidery, we will say a few words as to the frame itself, the manner of stretching the material in it, and the best and least fatiguing method of working at it.

The essential parts of an embroidery frame are : first, the bars, which have stout webbing nailed along them, and mortice holes at the ends ; second, the stretchers, which are usually flat pieces of wood, furnished with holes at the ends to allow of their being fastened by metal pegs into the mortice holes of the bars when the work is stretched.

In some cases the stretchers are fastened into the bars by strong iron screws, which are held by nuts.

FRAMING.

In choosing a frame for a piece of embroidery we must see that the webbing attached to the sides of the bar is long enough to take the work in one direction. Begin by

D

sewing the edge of the material closely with strong linen thread on to this webbing. If the work is too long to be put into the frame at one time (as in the case of borders for curtains, table-covers, &c.), all but the portion about to be worked should be rolled round one bar of the frame, putting silver paper and a piece of wadding between the material and the wood, so as to prevent its being marked.

The stretchers should then be put in and secured with the metal pegs.

A piece of the webbing having been previously stitched on to the sides of the material, it should now be braced with twine by means of a packing needle, passing the string over the stretchers between each stitch taken in the webbing, and, finally, drawing up the bracing until the material is strained evenly and tightly in the frame.

If the fabric is one which stretches easily, the bracings should not be drawn too tightly.

For small pieces of work a deal hand-frame, morticed at the corners, will suffice, and this may be rested on the table before the worker, being held in its position by two heavy leaden weights, covered with leather or baize, in order to prevent them from slipping. It should be raised off the table to a convenient height, thus saving the worker from stooping over her frame, which tires the eyes, and causes the blood to flow to the head.

There is no doubt that a well-made standing-frame is a great convenience, as its position need not be disturbed, and it can be easily covered up and put aside when not in use. It requires, however, to be very well made, and should, if possible, be of oak or mahogany, or it will warp and get out of order. It must also be well weighted to keep it steady.

For a large piece of work it is necessary to have a long heavy frame with wooden trestles, on which to rest it. The trestles should be made so as to enable the frame to be raised or lowered at will.

A new frame has recently been invented and is sold by the Royal School, which, being made with hinges and small upright pins, holds the ends of the material firmly, so that it can be rolled round and round the bar of the frame without the trouble of sewing it on to the webbing.

When a frame is not in use, care should be taken that it does not become warped from being kept in too dry or too hot a place, as it is then difficult to frame the work satisfactorily.

It will be found useful to have a small basket, lined with holland or silk, fastened to the side of the frame, to hold the silks, thimbles, scissors, &c., needed for the work. Two thimbles should be used, one on each hand, and the best are old silver or gold ones, with all the roughness worn off, or ivory or vulcanite.

The worker ought to wear a large apron with a bib to save her dress, and a pair of linen sleeves to prevent the cuffs from fraying or soiling her work.

Surgeon's bent scissors are useful for frame embroidery, but they are not necessary, as ordinary sharp-pointed scissors will answer every purpose.

When silk, satin, or velvet is not strong enough to bear the strain of framing and embroidering, it must be backed with a fine cotton or linen lining. The "backing" in this case is first framed, as described above, and the velvet or satin must then be laid on it, and first fastened down with pins; then sewn down with herringbone stitch, taking care that it is kept perfectly even with the thread of the "backing," and not allowed to wrinkle or blister.

It is most important that a worker should learn to use equally both hands, keeping the right hand above the frame till the arm is tired, then letting the left take its place while the right goes below.

A cover should be made large enough to envelop both the upper and under portions of the work, and to be fastened down to the sides, so as to protect it from dust when it is not being used, and during work it should be kept over the portion of the embroidery not actually in hand.

Lastly, a good light should be chosen, so as not to try the eyes.

Many materials can only be embroidered in a frame, and most work is best so done. A greater variety of stitches is possible, and on the stretched flat surface the worker can see the whole picture at once, and judge of the effect of the colours and shading as she carries out the design. It is the difference between drawing on stretched or crumpled paper.

CHAPTER V.

STITCHES USED IN FRAME EMBROIDERY.

Feather Stitch.—In framework, as in handwork, we restore the ancient name of *Feather work* or stitch— *Opus Plumarium.* We have already said that it was so-called from its likeness to the plumage of a bird.

This comes from the even lie of the stitches, which fit into and appear to overlap each other, presenting thus a marked contrast to the granulated effect of tent stitches, and the long ridges of the *Opus Anglicum,* having no hard lines as in stem stitch, or flat surfaces as in satin stitch.

Feather stitch, when worked in a frame, is exactly the same as that worked in the hand, except that it is more even and smooth. The needle is taken backwards and forwards through the material in stitches of varying lengths; the next row always fitting into the vacant spaces and projecting beyond them, so as to prepare for the following row.

Every possible gradation of colour can be effected in

this way, and it applies to every form of design—floral
or arabesque.   Natural flowers have mostly been worked
in this stitch.

A skilful embroiderer will be careful not to waste more
silk than is absolutely necessary on the back of the work,
while, at the same time, she will not sacrifice the artistic
effect by being too sparing of her back stitches.

"COUCHING," OR LAID EMBROIDERY.

THIS name is properly applied to all forms of embroidery in which the threads of crewel, silk, or gold are laid on the surface, and stitched on to it by threads coming from the back of the material. Under this head may be classed as varieties the ordinary "laid backgrounds," "diaper couchings," "brick stitch," "basket stitch," and the various forms of stuffed couchings which are found in ancient embroideries. Couching outlines are usually thick strands of double crewel, tapestry wool, filoselle, cord, or narrow ribbon laid down and stitched at regular intervals by threads crossing the couching line at right angles. They are used for coarse outline work, or for finishing the edges of appliqué.

Plain Couching, or "*Laid Embroidery*."—The threads are first laid evenly and straight from side to side of the space to be filled in, whether in the direction of warp or woof depends on the pattern ; the needle being passed through to the back, and brought up again not quite

close, but at a sufficient distance to allow of an intermediate stitch being taken backwards ; thus the threads
would be laid alternately first, third, second, fourth, and
so on. This gives a better purchase at each end than if
they were laid consecutively in a straight line. If the
line slants much, it is not necessary to alternate the rows.
When the layer is complete, threads of metal, or of the
same or different colour and texture, are laid across at
regular intervals, and are fixed down by stitches from the
back.

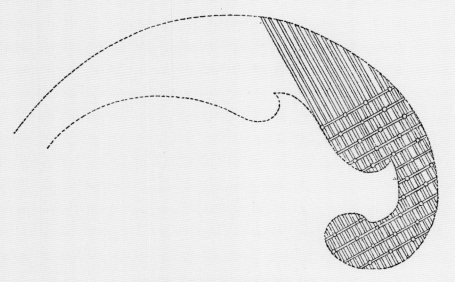

No. 11.—Plain Couching.

The beauty of this work depends upon its regularity.

This kind of embroidery, which we find amongst the
old Spanish, Cretan, and Italian specimens, is very useful
where broad, flat effects without shading are required ;
but unless it is very closely stitched down, it is not durable

if there is any risk of its being exposed to rough usage. It is possible to obtain very fine effects of colour in this style of work, as was seen in the old Venetian curtains transferred and copied for Louisa, Lady Ashburton. These were shown at the time of the Exhibition of Ancient Needlework at the School in 1878.

Ancient embroidery can be beautifully restored by grounding in "laid work," instead of transferring it where the ground is frayed, and the work is worthy of pre-servation. It must be stretched on a new backing, the frayed material carefully cut away, and the new ground couched as we have described.

In other varieties of couching, under which come the many forms of diapering, the threads are "laid" in the same manner as for ordinary couching; but in place of laying couching lines across these, the threads of the first layer are simply stitched down from the back, frequently with threads of another colour.

Net-patterned Couching.—The fastening stitches are placed diagonally instead of at right angles, forming a network, and are kept in place by a cross-stitch at each intersection.

This style of couching was commonly used as a ground in ecclesiastical work of the fourteenth and fifteenth centuries.

Brick Stitch.—The threads are laid down two together, and are stitched across at regular intervals. The next two threads are then placed together by the side, the fastening stitches being taken at the same distance from each other, but so as to occur exactly between the previous couplings. Thus giving the effect of brickwork.

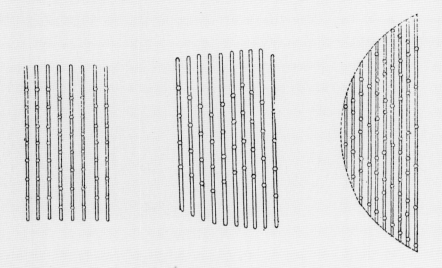

No. 12.—Three Illustrations of Diaper Couchings.

Diaper Couchings.—By varying the position of the fastening stitches different patterns may be produced, such as diagonal crossings, diamonds, zigzags, curves, &c.

They are properly all gold stitches; but purse silk, thin cord, or even untwisted silk may be used.

A wonderful example of the many varieties of diapering is to be seen in the South Kensington Museum, No. 689. It is modern Belgian work, executed for the Paris Exhibition of 1867. As a specimen of fine and beautiful diapering in gold, this could scarcely be surpassed.

Basket Stitch is one of the richest and most ornamental of these ancient modes of couching. Rows of "stuffing," manufactured in the form of soft cotton cord, are laid across the pattern and firmly secured.   Across these are placed gold threads, two at a time, and these are stitched down over each two rows of stuffing.   The two gold threads are turned at the edge of the pattern, and brought back close to the last, and fastened in the same way.   Three double rows of gold may be stitched over the same two rows of stuffing.

The next three rows must be treated as brick stitch, and fastened exactly between the previous stitchings, and so on, until the whole space to be worked is closely covered with what appears to be a golden wicker-work.

Strong silk must be used for the stitching.

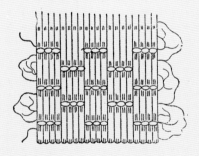

No. 13.—BASKET STITCH.

The Spanish School of Embroidery has always been famed for its excellence in this style, and has never lost the art.   The "Embroiderers of the King," as they are called, still turn out splendid specimens of this heavy and elaborate work, which are used for the gorgeous trappings of the horses of the nobility on gala days and state occasions.

A beautiful specimen was exhibited at the Royal School of Art-Needlework, in 1878, by the Countess Brownlow, of an altar-hanging, entirely worked in basket stitch, in gold on white satin, and a modern example is still to be seen at the School in a large counterpane, which was worked for the Philadelphia Exhibition from an ancient one also belonging to Lady Brownlow.

The Spanish embroiderers used these forms of couching over stuffing with coloured silks as well as gold, and produced wonderfully rich effects. One quilt exhibited by Mrs. Alfred Morrison in 1878 was a marvel of colouring and workmanship.

Basket stitch is mostly used now for church embroidery, or for small articles of luxury, such as ornamental pockets, caskets, &c.

Diapering is generally employed in the drapery of small figures, and in ecclesiastical work.

Many fabrics are manufactured in imitation of the older diapered backgrounds, and are largely used to replace them. Among these are the material known as silk brocatine, and several kinds of cloth of gold mentioned in our list of materials.

CUSHION STITCHES.

Cushion Stitch—the ancient *Opus Pulvinarium* of the Middle Ages, likewise called "Cross Stitch"—may lay claim to be one of the most ancient known in embroidery. There have been many varieties, but the principle is the same in all. It is worked on and through canvas, of which the threads, as in tapestry, regulate the stitches.

After six centuries of popularity it finally died out within the last few years as "Berlin wool work;" but will doubtless be revived again in some form after a time, as being well fitted for covering furniture on account of its firmness and durability.

In Germany and Russia it is still much used for embroidering conventional designs on linen ; and the beautiful Cretan and Persian work of which so much has lately been in the market, is executed in this style.

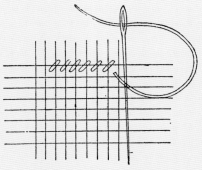

No. 14.—Tent Stitch.

Tent Stitch may be placed first under this class, in

which the thread coming from beneath is carried over
a single cross of the warp and woof of the canvas.

Simple Cross Stitch.—The worsted or silk is brought

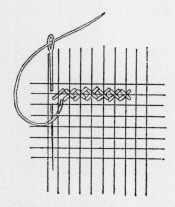

No. 15.—SIMPLE CROSS STITCH.

up again to the surface, one thread to the left of the spot
where the needle was inserted, and is crossed over the
first or "tent" stitch, forming a regular and even cross on
the surface.

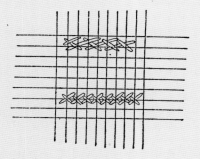

No. 16.—PERSIAN CROSS STITCH.

Persian Cross Stitch.—The peculiarity of this stitch is
that in the first instance the silk or worsted is carried

across two threads of the canvas ground, and is brought up in the intermediate space. It is then crossed over the latter half of the original stitch, and a fresh start is made.

Much of the beauty of Persian embroidery is produced by the irregularity of the crossing; the stitches being taken in masses, in any direction that seems most suitable to the design in hand, instead of being placed in regular rows, with the stitches all sloping in one direction, as is the case with the modern "Berlin work," this, with the happy choice of colours for which the Persians are so justly famous, produces a singular richness of effect.

Allied to these canvas stitches and having their origin in them, are the numerous forms of groundings, which are now worked on coarse linens, or in fact on any fabric; and have sometimes, although incorrectly, been called darning stitches, probably from their resemblance to the patterns which are found on samplers, for darning stockings, old table linen, &c. &c. Almost any pattern can be produced in this style of embroidery, simply by varying the relative length of the stitches.

Following the nomenclature of the committee which named and catalogued the specimens of ancient needlework exhibited in the South Kensington Museum in 1872, we have classed all the varieties of these grounding stitches under the name of Cushion stitch.

Cushion Stitches are taken as in laid embroidery, so as to leave all the silk and crewel on the surface, and only a single thread of the ground is taken up; but in place of lying in long lines, from end to end of the material, they are of even length, and are taken in a pattern, such as a waved line or zigzag ; so that when finished the ground presents the appearance of a woven fabric.

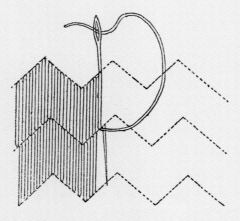

No. 17.—Cushion Stitch.

We give an illustration of one variety of cushion stitch, which may either be worked as described here, or in the hand, as in the woodcut.

A good modern example of this background was exhibited in the School, on a bed-hanging, worked for the Honourable Mrs. Percy Wyndham, from a design by Mr. W. Morris. In the Exhibition of Ancient Needlework last year were many beautiful specimens : notably one enormous wall-hanging of Italian seventeenth-century work, lent by Earl Spencer. Many of the fabrics known as "Tapestries" are woven imitations of these grounds, and carry embroidery so perfectly, that on the whole, except for small pieces, it seems a waste of hand-labour to work them in, as the effect is not very far removed from that of woven material, while the expense is, of course, very much greater.

The ancient specimens of this stitch are worked on a coarse canvas, differing greatly from that which was recently used for Berlin wool work.

It cannot now be obtained except by having it especially made to order. It has been replaced by a coarse hand-woven linen for the use of the School, but the ancient canvas is vastly superior, as its looseness makes it easier for the worker to keep her stitches in regular lines.

In some ancient specimens the design is worked in feather stitch, and the whole ground in cushion stitch. In others the design is in fine cross or tent stitch. There are several very beautiful examples of this kind of embroidery in the South Kensington Museum—Italian, of the seventeenth century.

A variety of cushion stitch, which we frequently see in old Italian embroideries, was taught in the Royal School of Art-Needlework by Miss Burden, and used under her direction in working flesh in some large figures designed by Mr. Walter Crane for wall decoration, and exhibited at the Centennial Exhibition at Philadelphia. The stitches are kept of one uniform length across the design. The next row is started from half the depth of the preceding stitch and kept of the same length throughout. Its beauty consists in its perfect regularity. If worked in the hand, the needle is brought back underneath the material as in satin stitch; but in the frame all the silk or worsted can be worked on the surface, with the exception of the small fastening stitches.

The effect when finished is that of a woven fabric.

It is really more suitable in its original character of a ground stitch than for working flesh. We have given an

E

illustration of it, because we are so frequently asked to describe " Burden stitch."

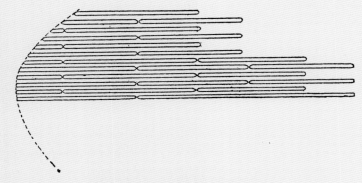

No. 18.—" BURDEN " STITCH.

This form of cushion stitch worked extremely fine has been used for flesh in very ancient embroideries, even before the introduction of the *Opus Anglicanum*, and is found in the works of the Flemish, German, Italian, and French schools of the fourteenth and fifteenth centuries.

It seems to have been worked in a frame on fine canvas, or on a fabric of very even threads, and the stitches so taken that the same amount of silk appears on the back as on the surface of the embroidery.

In a toilet cover of ancient Spanish work recently added to the South Kensington Museum, the design is entirely embroidered in varieties of *cushion stitch* in black floss silk upon a white linen ground. It is, however, extremely rare to see this stitch used in any other way than as a ground, except in actual canvas work; in which we often see varieties of it used to fill in portions of the design, while another stitch will be devoted entirely to the grounding.

These stitches were often executed on an open net.

Stem Stitch is used in frame embroidery, and does not differ in any way from that described at page 20, under "handwork," except that the needle is of course worked through the material with both hands, as is the case in all frame work.

The same may be said of "split stitch;" but this is more frequently (because more easily) worked in a frame than done in the hand.

Japanese Stitch is a modification of stem, but its peculiarity consists in the worker taking very long stitches, and then bringing the needle back to within a short distance of the first starting-place; so that they may be in even parallel lines, advancing by gradation from left to right. It is principally used for working water or ground in a landscape.

No. 19.

Tambour Work has fallen into disuse, but was greatly admired when our grandmothers in the last century sprigged Indian muslins or silks with coloured flowers for dresses, and copied or adapted Indian designs on fine linen coverlets. These were very refined, but no more effective than a good chintz. There are exquisite specimens of the stitch to be seen in most English homes, and in France it was in vogue in the days of Marie Antoinette. Its use is now almost confined to the manufacture of what is known as Irish or Limerick lace, which is made on net in the old tambour frames, and with a tambour or crochet hook. The frame is formed of two rings of wood or iron, made to fit loosely one within the other. Both rings are covered with baize or flannel wound round them till the inner one can only just be passed through the outer. The fabric to be embroidered is placed over the smaller hoop, and the other is pressed down over it and firmly fixed with a screw. A small wooden frame of this description is universally used in Ireland for white embroidery on linen or muslin. In tambour work the thread is kept below the frame and guided by the left hand, while the hook or crochet needle is passed from the surface through the fabric, and brings up a loop of the thread through the preceding stitch, and the needle again inserted, forming thus a close chain on the surface of the work.

The difficulty of working chain stitch in a frame probably led to the introduction of a hook for this class of embroidery.

Perhaps we ought not to omit all mention of the *Opus Anglicum* or *Anglicanum* (English work), though it is strictly ecclesiastical, and therefore does not enter into our province.

Dr. Rock[1] and other authorities agree in thinking that the distinctive feature of this style, which was introduced about the end of the thirteenth century, was a new way of working the flesh in subjects containing figures.

[1] See Dr. Rock's preface to his " Descriptive Catalogue of TEXTILE FABRICS " in the Kensington Museum.

Instead of the faces being worked in rows of straight stitches (like that described as Burden stitch on page 49) as we see in the old Flemish, German, and Italian work of the same period, the English embroiderers invented a new stitch, which they commenced in the centre of the cheek and worked round and round—gradually letting the lines fall into outer circles of ordinary feather stitch.

Having thus prepared an elastic surface, they proceeded to model the forms and make lights and shadows by pressing the work into hollows, with small heated metal balls, the work being probably damped as a preparation for this process. So skilfully did they carry out their intention, that the effect is still the same after the lapse of five centuries. We must unwillingly add that, though much appreciated in the thirteenth century, the effect is rather curious and quaint than beautiful.

The Syon cope in the Kensington Museum, of the thirteenth century, is a fine specimen of this attempt to give the effect of bas-relief to the sacred subjects depicted. The whole cope shows how various were the stitches worked at that period. On examination with a micro- scope, the flesh stitch appears to be merely a fine split stitch worked spirally, as we now work fruit.

CUT WORK OR APPLIQUÉ.

DECORATIVE cut work is of infinite variety, but may be divided into two groups, "inlaid appliqué" and "onlaid appliqué."

"*Inlaid*" appliqué consists in tracing the same pattern on two different fabrics, say a gold cloth and a crimson velvet ; then cutting both out carefully, and inlaying the gold flowers into the crimson velvet ground, and the crimson flowers into the gold ground.

This kind of work may be seen constantly in Italian rooms of the seventeenth century, and the alternate breadths of crimson and gold give a very fine effect as of pilasters, and in general are enriched by a valance applied at the top, and a plain border at the bottom.

The *inlaid* part is sewn down with thread, and covered with cord or couchings of floss silk. Sometimes narrow ribbons or fine strips of cut silk are stitched over the edges to keep them down flat.

" *Onlaid* appliqué" is done by cutting out the pattern in one or many coloured materials, and laying it down on an intact ground of another material. Parts are often shaded with a brush, high lights and details worked in with stitches of silk, and sometimes whole flowers or figures are embroidered, cut out, and couched down. This sort of work is extremely amusing, and gives scope to much play of fancy and ingenuity, and when artistically composed it is sometimes very beautiful.

Another style of " onlaid appliqué " is only worked in solid outlines, laid down in ribbon or cord, sometimes in

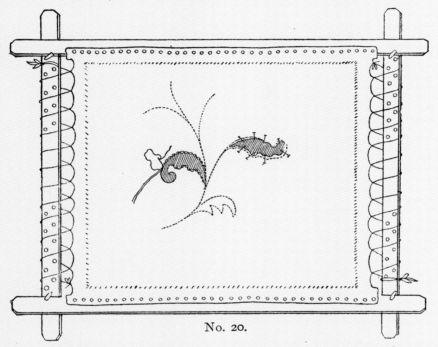

No. 20.

both. This was much in vogue in the time of Queen Anne, and for a hundred years after.

The ribbon, very soft and thick, sometimes figured, sometimes plain, was manufactured with a stout thread on each side, which could be drawn, and so regulate the ribbon and enable it to follow the flow of the pattern.

The German, French, and Italians often enriched this style of work with a flower, embroidered and applied thrown in here and there. Very small fringes also were introduced into the pattern, or arabesqued.

" Cut work," like the appellation " Feather stitch," has a totally different meaning when it is given to white embroidery, and it has nothing to do with appliqué, but takes its name from the fact that the pattern is mostly cut or punched out, and then edged with button-hole or plain overlaid stitch.

In working appliqué it is best, although not absolutely necessary, to have the design traced on the material to be used as a ground, which must then be framed as for ordinary embroidery.   A copy of the design must be made on tracing-paper, and the outlines carefully pricked out with a needle or pin, laying the paper on several folds of flannel or cloth for greater convenience in pricking.

A pad, made of a long strip of flannel about four inches wide, rolled very tightly, must be made ready, and some pounce made of about equal quantities of finely powdered charcoal and pipe-clay.   The leaf or scroll which is wanted for the work must now be selected, and the pricked design laid face downwards on the fabric which is to be applied.   The flannel pad must be dipped in the pounce and rubbed well into the outlines of the pricked design, which must be held firmly in its place with the left hand.   On lifting the tracing-paper, the design will be found to be marked out on the material distinctly enough for it to be cut out with a sharp pair of scissors. The pounce can afterwards be dusted off. .

The leaf or scroll having been thus cut out must be fastened in its place on the design with small pins, and then carefully sewn down.   The edges are then finished off by stitches of embroidery or by a couching line (*see* page 39).   The stems are frequently worked in with stem stitching or couching, and the leaves enriched by large veinings of crewel or silk work, or in conventional designs, with some of the many varieties of herringboning.

Gold Embroidery on velvet or satin grounds requires to be worked on a strong even linen, and then cut out and applied in the same manner as ordinary appliqué. Where a particularly rich and raised effect is required any embroidery may be treated in this manner. It is of course more troublesome, but quite repays the labour spent upon it by the increased beauty of the work.

The transfer of old embroideries on to a new ground is usually done by appliqué, although we have already described a better process at page 39.

In transferring old needlework it is necessary to cut away the ground close to the edge of the embroidery. It is then placed on the new material, which has been previously framed, and the outline tacked down. The best way of finishing is then to work in the edges with silks *dyed exactly to match* the colours in the old work. If properly done, it is impossible to discover which are old and which new stitches, and only by examining the back, that the work has been transferred at all.

We used the words "*dyed to match*" advisedly, as it is impossible otherwise to procure new silks which will correspond with the old.

Embroidery transferred in this manner is as good as it was in its first days, and in many cases is much better, for time often has the same mellowing and beautifying effect in embroideries as in paintings.

A less expensive, but also a much less charming,

method is to edge the old embroidery after applying it
to the new ground with a cord or line of couching.

With this treatment it is, however, always easy to
perceive that the work has been transferred.

For almost all kinds of appliqué it is necessary to back
the material ; and it is done in this manner :—

A piece of thin cotton or linen fabric is stretched
tightly on to a board with tacks or drawing-pins. It is
then covered smoothly, and completely, with paste. The
wrong side of the velvet, satin, serge, or whatever is to be
used in the work, is then pressed firmly down on the
pasted surface with the hands, and then left to dry.

In giving the foregoing account of the most typical
stitches, we hope we have succeeded in showing the
principle on which each should be worked. They form
the basis of all embroidery, and their numerous modifi-
cations cannot be fully discussed in the limit we have
prescribed to ourselves. It is sufficient to observe that
the instruction we have tried to impart is that which it is
absolutely necessary for the needleworker to master
thoroughly before she attempts to cope with the artistic
element of her work. That it is a creative art is un-
doubted, for no two pieces of embroidery are alike unless
executed by the same hand, and from the same design.

For the advanced artist there is a store of instruction
in the fine collection at South Kensington, which, seen
by the light of Dr. Rock's invaluable " Catalogue of
Textile Fabrics," is an education in itself, of which the
ethnological as well as the artistic interest cannot be
over-estimated, and it is within the reach of all who can
find time to bestow upon it.

STRETCHING AND FINISHING.

ALWAYS avoid using an iron to embroidery. It flattens the work, and is apt to injure the colour. For embroidery on linen, unless very badly done, it will be found quite sufficient to stretch the work as tightly as possible with white tacks or drawing-pins on a clean board, and damp it evenly with a sponge. Leave it until quite dry, and then unfasten it, and, if necessary, comb out the fringe. If it is new work, it should not be fringed until after it has been stretched.

For crewel work on cloth or serge, it is sometimes necessary to rub a little shoemaker's paste on to the back of the embroidery, while it is tightly stretched. When pasting can be avoided, it is always better to do without it ; but it serves to steady the work in some cases, and makes it wear better. Unless it is absolutely necessary, it is better not to paste the back of screen panels, whatever may be the materials on which they are worked ; but more especially satin or velvet, as it interferes with the straining of the work by the cabinet-maker.

We give a recipe for EMBROIDERY PASTE, which is said to be excellent :—Three and a half spoonfuls of flour, and as much powdered resin as will lie on a half-penny. Mix these well and smoothly with half a pint of water, and pour it into an iron saucepan. Put in one teaspoonful of essence of cloves, and go on stirring till it boils.   Let it boil for five minutes, and turn it into a gallipot to cool.

N.B.—Let the gallipot have in it a muslin bag: the water can then be drained out from time to time, and the paste will be much better.

CLEANING.

GOOD crewels will always wash or clean without injury; but the cheap and inferior worsteds will not do so.   Ordinary crewel work on linen may be washed at home, by plunging it into a lather made by water in which bran has been boiled, or even with simple soap-suds, so long as no soda or washing-powder is used.   It should be carefully rinsed without wringing, and hung up to dry. When almost dry, it may be stretched out with drawing-pins on a board, and will not require ironing.

Embroidery on cloth or serge may often be cleaned with benzoline, applied with a piece of clean flannel; but in any case, where a piece of work is much soiled, or in the case of fine d'oyleys, it is safer to send it to the cleaner's.

Messrs. Pullar and Son, Perth Dye Works, are very successful in cleaning all kinds of embroidery without injuring it.

In many cases it may be well dyed—the silk in which the design is worked always showing a different shade from the ground.

APPENDIX.

DESIGNS FOR EMBROIDERY.

DESCRIPTION OF THE PLATES.

No. 1.—DESIGN FOR WALL-PANEL.   By Mr. E. Burne Jones.

Worked in outline on neutral-tinted hand-woven linen in brown crewel. This style of embroidery is very suitable for internal decoration, where a good broad effect is required without a large amount of labour.   A frieze or dado, or complete panelling of a room, may be worked in this way at a comparatively small cost.

No. 2.—DESIGN FOR WALL OR SCREEN PANEL.   By Mr. Walter Crane.   Representing the Four Elements.

Embroidered in crewels on a silk ground of dead gold colour partly outlined.

No. 3.—DESIGN FOR QUILT OR TABLE COVER.   By Mr. George Aitchison.

A border of sunflowers and pomegranates, with powderings of the same for the centre.

This has been embroidered on cream-coloured satin de chine in solid crewel work, with charming effect, both for a counterpane and curtains.

No. 4.—DESIGN FOR WALL PANELLING OR CURTAINS. By Mr. Fairfax Wade.

To be worked in outline and solid embroidery, in silk or filoselle, on satin de chine.

No. 5.—DESIGN FOR QUILT OR COUVRE PIED. By Mr. Fairfax Wade. To introduce squares of Greek or guipure lace.

Worked in golden shades of silk on linen, lined with silk of the same colour. The embroidery is partly solid and partly outline, very fine and delicate.

No. 6.—DESIGN FOR SOFA-BACK COVER. By Mr. W. Morris.

Worked on hand-woven linen in two shades of gold-coloured silks. Outline.

No. 7.—DESIGN FOR SOFA-BACK COVER OR PIANO PANEL. By Mr. George Aitchison.

Worked in two shades of blue silk on hand-woven linen or satin de chine.

No. 8.—DESIGN FOR APPLIQUÉ. By Mr. Fairfax Wade.

Nos. 9 and 10. — DESIGNS FOR CHAIR-SEATS OR CUSHIONS. By Miss Jekyll. Periwinkle and Iris.

No. 11.—DESIGN FOR BORDER. By Miss Webster. To be worked in outline in silk or crewel.

No. 12.—DESIGN FOR BORDER FOR CURTAIN OR TABLE COVER. Designed by Miss Burnside, of the R.S.A.N.

No. 13.—TABLE BORDER. Designed by Mr. Fairfax Wade. Conventional Buttercup. To be worked either solid or in outline.

No. 14.—TABLE BORDER. Designed by Mr. Walter Crane. For solid embroidery in crewel or silk.

No. 15.—TABLE BORDER. Designed by Mr. Walter Crane. For solid embroidery in crewel or silk.

No. 16.—BORDER. Designed by Miss Mary Herbert, R.S.A.N. For crewel or silk embroidery, either in outline or solid.

No. 17.—TWO PANELS. Designed by Rev. Selwyn Image. Representing Juno and Minerva.

No. 18.—TWO PANELS. Designed by Rev. Selwyn Image. Representing Venus and Proserpine. To be worked in outline on linen, as No. 1, or in coloured silks on a groundwork of satin de chine.

No. 19.—WALL HANGING. Designed by Mr. W. Morris. To be worked on linen in outline.

No. 20.—WALL HANGING. Designed by Mr. W. Morris. Worked on linen. Background in Silk Cushion Stitch.

No. 21.—BORDER FOR APPLIQUÉ. Copied from Ancient Italian work.

No. 22.—ITALIAN DESIGN. A Specimen. Showing the application of transposed Appliqué.

1. DESIGN FOR WALL PANEL.

By E. Burne-Jones.

2. DESIGN FOR WALL PANEL
By Walter Crane.

Vincent Brooks Day & Son, Lith.

3. DESIGN FOR A QUILT OR TABLE COVER.
By George Aitchison.

4. DESIGN FOR WALL PANEL OR CURTAIN.   *By Fairfax Wade.*

5. DESIGN FOR A QUILT OR COUVRE-PIED.
By Fairfax Wade.

6. DESIGN FOR A SOFA-BACK COVER. *By William Morris.*

7. DESIGN FOR A SOFA-BACK COVER OR PIANO PANEL. *By George Aitchison.*

Vincent Brooks Day & Son, Lith.

8. DESIGN FOR APPLIQUÉ. *By Fairfax Wade.*

DESIGNS FOR CHAIR-SEATS OR CUSHIONS. (9. PERIWINKLE 10. IRIS.) *By Miss Jekyll.*

Vincent Brooks Day & Son, Lith.

12. DESIGN FOR A BORDER FOR A CURTAIN OR TABLE COVER. *By Miss Burnside.*

Vincent Brooks Day & Son. Lith.

11. DESIGN FOR A BORDER. *By Miss Webster.*

DESIGNS FOR TABLE BORDERS.
No. 13 *by Fairfax Wade;* 14 *and* 15 *by Walter Crane;* 16 *by Mary Herbert.*

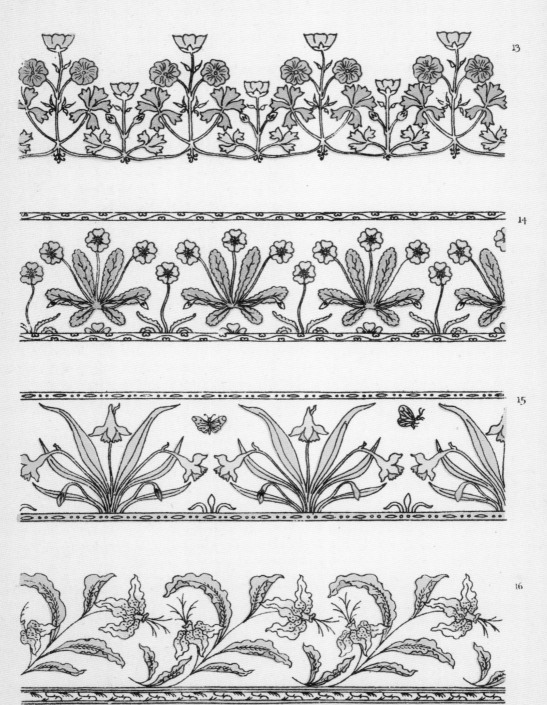

17.   TWO DESIGNS FOR WALL PANELS—"JUNO" AND "MINERVA."
By the Rev. Selwyn Image.

18. TWO DESIGNS FOR WALL PANELS—"VENUS" AND "PROSERPINE."
By the Rev. Selwyn Image.

19. DESIGN FOR WALL-HANGING.
By William Morris.

Vincent Brooks Day & Son, Lith.

25. DESIGN FOR WALL-HANGING.
By William Morris.

21. DESIGN FOR BORDER FOR APPLIQUÉ.
From Ancient Italian Work.

Vincent Brooks Day & Son, Lith.

22. ITALIAN DESIGN.

Showing the application of transposed Appliqué.

Royal School of Art-Needlework.

Incorporated under "The Companies' Acts, 1862 and 1867," by licence of the Board of Trade, granted under 30 and 31 Vic., c. 131, sec. 23.

Share Capital, £10,000, in 1000 Shares of £10 each. Debenture Capital, £10,000, to be issued in Debentures of £50 each.

Patrons.

HER MAJESTY THE QUEEN.

H.R.H. THE PRINCE OF WALES.

H.R.H. THE PRINCESS OF WALES.

President.

H.R.H. THE PRINCESS CHRISTIAN OF SCHLESWIG-HOLSTEIN.
Princess of Great Britain and Ireland.

Vice-President.

THE LADY MARIAN ALFORD.

Managing Committee.

THE COUNTESS SPENCER.	THE HON. LADY WELBY GREGORY.
THE COUNTESS COWPER.	THE HON. MRS. PERCY WYND-HAM.
THE COUNTESS BROWNLOW.	
THE VISCOUNTESS DOWNE.	
THE LADY SARAH SPENCER.	MRS. EDWARD BARING.

(*With power to add to their number.*)

Honorary Members of the Managing Committee.

THE LADY CHARLOTTE SCHREIBER.	THE LADY FITZHARDINGE.
THE HON. LADY HAMILTON-GORDON.	THE HON. MRS. STUART WORTLEY.

F

Finance Committee.

THE DUKE OF WESTMINSTER, K.G. | THE RIGHT HON. SIR WILLIAM
THE EARL BROWNLOW. | HENRY GREGORY, K.C.M.G.
THE LORD SUDELEY. | MICHAEL BIDDULPH, ESQ., M.P.
SIR COUTTS LINDSAY, BART. | EDMUND OLDFIELD, ESQ.

Bankers.

LONDON AND COUNTY BANK, Albert Gate Branch.

Solicitors.

MESSRS. TRINDERS & CURTIS-HAYWARD, 4, Bishopsgate Street
Within, E.C.

Offices.

EXHIBITION ROAD, SOUTH KENSINGTON.

PROSPECTUS.

The School was founded in 1872, under the Presidency of H.R.H. the Princess Christian of Schleswig-Holstein, for the twofold purpose of supplying suitable employment for Gentlewomen and restoring Ornamental Needlework to the high place it once held among the decorative arts.

It was first established, under the title of School of Art-Needlework, in Sloane Street; but in 1875 was removed to the present premises in the Exhibition Road, and Her Majesty the Queen was graciously pleased to grant to it the prefix of " Royal."

The Royal School of Art-Needlework exhibited at the Centennial Exhibition of Philadelphia, 1876, and received a Certificate of Award— medals not being granted to institutions or corporate bodies. A Silver Medal was also granted by the Jurors of the International Exhibition, Paris, 1878, for embroideries exhibited there.

The result of seven years' experience of the working of the School has shown that the objects for which it was formed are appreciated by the public, and has justified its establishment on a permanent basis. This has accordingly been effected under a special licence from the Board of

Trade, granted under authority of an Act of Parliament which authorizes the incorporation of associations *not* constituted for purposes of profit.

The ultimate profits of the Association, after payment of all Debentures, are to be applied to such charitable or other purposes as the Association may from time to time determine, not being inconsistent with the provisions of the Memorandum of Association, which require that the Shareholders shall not take any personal prcfit out of the Association.

The government of the School is vested in :

First.—A President, Vice-President, and General Council.

Second.—A Managing Committee to be selected from the General Council, except as to Honorary Members to be nominated by the Managing Committee.

Third.—A Finance Committee, of whom a majority are to be elected by the Shareholders, and the remainder nominated by the Managing Committee. The sanction of this Committee is required for all expenditure.

Agencies have now been opened in Liverpool, Manchester, Leeds, Norwich, Birmingham and Glasgow ; and a member of the staff has been sent out to take charge of the School of Art-Needlework in Philadelphia.

The Show Rooms are open from 10 a.m. to 6 p.m. in Summer, and to 5 p.m. in Winter, and close on Saturdays at 2 p.m.

All letters must be addressed " The Secretary."

Lists of designs, prices of prepared and finished work, terms for lessons, and addresses of Provincial Agents, may be obtained by writing to the Secretary.

A Branch School for Scotland has now been opened in Glasgow. Show Rooms at 108, St. Vincent Street.

ROYAL SCHOOL OF ART-NEEDLEWORK,

EXHIBITION ROAD,

SOUTH KENSINGTON.

~~~~~~~~~~

PREPARED WORK.

Work can be obtained from the ROYAL SCHOOL OF ART-NEEDLE-WORK having a design traced, a portion of the embroidery commenced, and sufficient materials for finishing. Ladies' own materials will be traced and prepared for working if desired. Dresses must be cut out and tacked together before being sent to the School, and lines marked on the material to show where the design is to be placed.

When an order for prepared work is executed exactly by the directions given, or when the selection of Design or Colouring is left to the School, *the work cannot be exchanged or taken back.*

The materials supplied with the work are considered more than sufficient to finish it, and if more are required afterwards they must be purchased separately.

A few specimen prices are quoted, but *no estimates can be given for prepared work,* except in cases of large orders where a great quantity of material is supplied.

All Designs supplied are Copyright of the Royal School of Art-Needlework, and must not be made use of for purposes of sale.

Designs on paper are not supplied under any circumstances, nor can work be sent out on approbation.

All work supplied is stamped with the monogram of the ROYAL SCHOOL OF ART-NEEDLEWORK, as above, in addition to the letters P. W.

N.B.—*An extra charge is made for all designs not ordinarily used for Prepared Work.*

APPROXIMATE PRICES OF PREPARED WORK AND MATERIALS.

TABLE COVERS, on Diagonal, from £1 1s. to £5 5s.

,,   ,,   Serge   ,,   18s. to £3 3s.

LINEN TABLE COVERS, yard square, 14s. 6d. to £1 10s.

CHAIR BACK COVERS, Linen, 7s. 6d. to £1 1s.

BORDERS, on Linen, suitable for Table Covers or Dresses, from 5s. per yard.

BORDERS, on Serge or Diagonal, suitable for Table Covers or Dresses, from 7s. per yard.

BORDERS, on Serge or Diagonal, suitable for Curtains, Chimney Valances, &c., from 13s. per yard.

N.B.—*If several yards are ordered of one pattern the price is lower.*

BANNER SCREENS, Linen (various), 8s. 6d. to 15s. 6d.

,,   ,,   Diagonal, 12s. 6d. to £2 2s.

BABIES' BLANKETS, from 14s. 6d.

BATH BLANKETS, yard square, 17s. 6d. ; yard and a half square, 26s.

CHILDREN'S DRESS, from 18s. to £1 10s.

TENNIS APRONS, from £1 1s.

CUSHIONS, Linen, 7s. 6d. to 12s 6d. ; on Diagonal, &c., 10s. 6d. to £1 1s.

TOILET MATS or D'OYLEY, 8 inches square, from £1 6s. to £3 3s. per dozen.

FOLDING SCREENS, on Sailcloth, £1 1s. to £1 10s. per panel.

CREWELS.

Crewels are sold at the rate of 8*d*. per ounce skein, or in quarter-pound bundles, containing not more than four shades, at 2*s*.   In quarter-pound bundles, containing selected colours, at 3*s*.

EMBROIDERY SILKS, at 6*s*. 6*d*. per ounce reel, and 3*s*. 3*d*. per half-ounce reel of one shade ; or at 8*s*. per ounce of selected colours.

FILOSELLE, 3*s*. 6*d*. per ounce.

NEEDLES, 9*d*. per packet.

MATERIALS, suitable for embroidery, such as Homespuns, Fancy Linens, Serge, Diagonal, Utrecht Velvet, Satin de Chine, &c. &c., may be purchased at the School.

NOT LESS THAN ONE YARD SOLD.

LIST OF DESIGNS.

CHAIR BACKS.

Honeysuckle, Bramble, Poppy, Passion Flower, Taxonia, Wild Rose, Apple Blossom, Orange with Flowers, Virginia Creeper, Fish and Bulrushes, Winter Cherry, Corn Flower, Hops, Carnations, Cherry, Daisy Powdered, Primrose Powdered, Faust Motto, Iris Seed, Japanese, Jessamine, Lantern Plant, Periwinkle, Potato, Zynia, Tiger Lily, Geranium, Burrage, Corncockle, Hawthorn, Daffodil, Iris, Love-in-a-Mist, &c. &c., with many conventional designs.

NARROW BORDERS.

SUITABLE FOR DRESSES OR TABLE COVERS.

Love-in-a-Mist, Daisy, Poppy, Honeysuckle, Strawberry, Forget-me-Not, Flax, Jessamine, Blackberry, Virginia Creeper, Hawthorn, Daffodil, Cowslip, Cherry, Buttercup, Mountain Ash, Ragged Robin, Potentilla, Apple Blossom, Strawberry and Blossom, Christmas Rose, &c. &c., also many conventional designs.

CURTAIN BORDERS.

Sunflower, Pomegranate, Passion Flower, Taxonia, Poppy, Lilies, Magnolia, Orange, Hops, Marguerites, Love-in-a-Mist, Wild Rose, Arbutus, Chrysanthemum, Iris, Cowslip, Primrose, Apple, &c. &c.

The same Designs can be had in Horizontal Borders for Chimney Valances, wide Table Borders, and can be adapted for any purpose.

N.B.—The Royal School of Art-Needlework has no Branch School nor any Agency in London.

Royal School of Art-Needlework.

EXHIBITION ROAD, SOUTH KENSINGTON.

September, 1878.

The Committee of Management of the ROYAL SCHOOL OF ART-NEEDLEWORK has now organized Classes for Teaching Ornamental Needlework at their premises in the Exhibition Road, South Kensington.

These Classes are especially established for the instruction of Ladies and Children, and include every kind of stitch in Crewel, Silk, and Gold.

Ladies who wish to take lessons, or send their Children, are requested to send their names to the Secretary, who will inform them when to attend.

Each Course will consist of Six Lessons.

CREWELS.
THIRD CLASS—SIX LESSONS.

	£	s.	d.
One Person	1	4	0
Two of same Family	1	16	0
Three ditto	2	8	0

SILK AND APPLIQUÉ.
SECOND CLASS—SIX LESSONS.

	£	s.	d.
One Person	1	10	0
Two of same Family	2	5	0
Three ditto	3	0	0

ECCLESIASTICAL EMBROIDERY.
FIRST CLASS—SIX LESSONS.

	£	s.	d.
One Person	2	0	0
Two of same Family	3	0	0
Three ditto	4	0	0

SINGLE LESSONS.

	£	s.	d.
One single Lesson (for 1 hour) on Lesson day	0	7	0
Ditto ditto Special day	0	8	6
Ditto on Ecclesiastical Work (at any time)	0	10	6

Private Lessons at Home, 10s. 6d. the hour and expenses.

Special terms for Classes of Twelve and upwards.

FINISHED WORK.

CURTAIN BORDERS, on Serge or Diagonal Cloth, from £2 10s. to £10 10s., about 3½ yards long.

DRESS BORDERS, on ditto, from 7s. to 18s. per yard.

     „   „   on House Flannel, from 3s. 6d. to 10s. 6d. per yard.

CURTAIN BORDERS, on Linen, from £1 10s. to £6 6s. each.

TABLE BORDERS, on Linen, from £1 1s. to £2 10s.

CHAIR BACKS, on Linen, from 14s. 6d. to £2 10s.

SOFA BACKS, on Linen and Silk, from £2 2s. to £10.

TABLE COVERS, on Linen, from £1 3s. to £5.

     „   „   Serge, from £1 1s. to £7.

     „   „   Diagonal, from 30s. to £26.

SMALL CHAIR SEATS, on Diagonal, from 13s. to £2 12s.

LARGE   „   „   Serge, from 13s. to £3 3s.

CUSHIONS, made up, from £2 2s. to £5 7s.

CHILDREN'S DRESSES, from £1 1s. to £3 3s.

     „   APRONS, from 12s. 6d. to £1 1s.

CHILDREN'S FRENCH BLOUSES, 18s. 6d. to £2 3s.

LADIES' LAWN TENNIS APRONS, from £1 5s. to £3 10s.

LINEN D'OYLEYS, from £2 7s. to £8 8s. per dozen.

TEA COSIES, on Diagonal, from 16s. 6d.

KETTLEDRUM D'OYLEYS, each 5s. 6d. to 16s. 6d.

SACHETS, with Mat to correspond, on Linen, from £1 6s.

FOLDING SCREENS, from £13 to £100.

CURTAINS, on Serge or Linen, from £10 to £60 per pair.

MANTEL VALANCES, from £2 2s. to £10 10s.

BANNER SCREENS, from £1 10s.

COUNTERPANES, from £6 to £80.

TABLE SCREENS, from £4 4s.

LADIES' ALGERIAN HOODS, from £3 to £10.

FANS, Mounted, from £2 7s. to £20.

CARRIAGE RUGS, from £2 to £10.

BLOTTER AND ENVELOPE BOX, from £8 8s.

     „   on Linen, from £1 5s.

ENVELOPE BOX, on Linen, from £3.

PHOTOGRAPH FRAMES, from £1 10s.

BELLOWS, from £1 17s.
OPERA CLOAKS, from £3 3s.
NIGHTINGALE DRESSING JACKET, from £2.
BATH SLIPPERS, from 6s. 6d. per pair.
WASHSTAND BACKS, from £1 5s.
BLANKET MATS, for Bath, 15s. 6d.
BERCEAUNETTE COVERS, from £1 10s.
SUNSHADE COVERS, from £3 3s.
PIANO PANELS, from £1 3s.
BABIES' HEAD FLANNELS, from £1 3s.
    ,,   CLOAKS, from £4 4s.
HANDKERCHIEF SACHETS, from £3 3s.
KNITTING POCKETS, from £1 1s.

P. O. Orders Payable to L. HIGGIN, *Exhibition Road.   Not more than* 18 *Stamps received.*

AGENTS IN THE COUNTRY.

Liverpool : Messrs. RUMNEY & LOVE, Bold Street.
Manchester : Messrs. E. GOODALL & Co., King Street.
Leeds : Messrs. MARSH, JONES, & CRIBBS.
Norwich : Messrs. ROBERTSON & SONS, Queen Street.
Glasgow : Messrs. ALEXANDER & HOWELL, 108, St. Vincent Street.
Birmingham : Messrs. MANTON, SONS, & GILBERT.

And for

America : Messrs. TORREY, BRIGHT, & CAPEN, Boston

BRANCH SCHOOL FOR SCOTLAND :

116, ST. VINCENT STREET, GLASGOW.

All information to be obtained at the Show Rooms,
108, St. Vincent Street.

As advertisements have from time to time appeared in various newspapers offering for sale designs of the Royal School of Art-Needlework, the Public is requested to note that no designs either on pricked paper, or in any other form than on commenced work, are, or ever have been, sold by the School, or supplied to any agent. Further, that no tracing powder is used in preparing the patterns, or sold for that purpose. All designs, therefore, offered as those of the Royal School are either entirely spurious, or are pirated from theirs.

CHISWICK PRESS :—C. WHITTINGHAM, TOOKS COURT,
CHANCERY LANE.